Anatomy & Development of the
INDY CAR

Tony Sakkis

Motorbooks International
Publishers & Wholesalers ®

First published in 1994 by Motorbooks International Publishers & Wholesalers, PO Box 2, 729 Prospect Avenue, Osceola, WI 54020 USA

© Tony Sakkis, 1994

All rights reserved. With the exception of quoting brief passages for the purposes of review no part of this publication may be reproduced without prior written permission from the Publisher

Motorbooks International is a certified trademark, registered with the United States Patent Office

The information in this book is true and complete to the best of our knowledge. All recommendations are made without any guarantee on the part of the author or Publisher, who also disclaim any liability incurred in connection with the use of this data or specific details

We recognize that some words, model names and designations, for example, mentioned herein are the property of the trademark holder. We use them for identification purposes only. This is not an official publication

Motorbooks International books are also available at discounts in bulk quantity for industrial or sales-promotional use. For details write to Special Sales Manager at the Publisher's address

Library of Congress Cataloging-in-Publication Data Available

ISBN 0-87938-874-9

On the front cover: 1993 Indianapolis 500 winner Emerson Fittipaldi throttles his Chevrolet-powered Penske around the oval at Phoenix in the 1993 Valvoline 200. *Richard Dole*

On the title page: Teo Fabi tests in the 1994 Pennzoil Special, a Reynard chassis with a new Ilmor D engine. *Deke Holgate, Pennzoil Public Relations*

On the back cover: A.J. Foyt smiles after qualifying for the 1967 Indy 500, which he won (*courtesy Goodyear*); Robby Gordon drove A.J. Foyt's Indy Car in 1993 (*courtesy Copenhagen Racing*); A Chevrolet-Ilmore engine is wheeled into the garage area; and the inner workings of a modern Indy Car's front end.

Unless otherwise noted, all photos are by Ray Touriel, John Overholtzer, and Tony Sakkis

Printed and bound in the United States of America

Contents

Acknowledgments

Writing a book is nothing more than collecting data and putting it down on paper. If I were an expert on the things about which I've written, I'd be in the business of designing race cars instead of writing books about them. The acknowledgments are more than just thank-yous; they convey the admiration and signify the deep respect I have for each person who helped me collect my data. I both thank them and apologize at the same time for asking so much of them.

Thanks to Mario Andretti, Gary Armentrout, Randy Bain, Brian Barnhardt, Ian Bisco, Susan Bradshaw, Eddie Cheever, John Chuhran, Dave Cornwell, Kevin Diamond, Dominic Dobson, Dave Elshoff, Emerson Fittipaldi, Jim Hall, Alex Hering, Robin Herring, Deke Holgate, Steve Horne, Kevin Kennedy, Michael Kranefuss, Randy Lewis, Arie Luyendyk, John Love, Nigel Mansell, Rick Mears, Leo Mehl, Jim Morton, John Overholtzer, Paul Ray, Bobby Rahal, Wally Reese, Scott Sharp, Danny Sullivan, Al Unser, Jr., Mike Wolther, and John Zamanski.

Special thanks to Marc Spiegel, who answered my requests with embarrassing speed, and who did much more for me than he could ever know. One of the good guys

Introduction

When I began gathering information for *The Anatomy and Development of an Indy Car*, I had an idea in mind of what an Indy car was. As I had always seen it, an Indy Car was a chassis first, an engine second, and perhaps a variety of components—all in what seemed to be various stages of anarchy and which were somehow integrated into a whole piece—an Indy Car. To me, it was another race car, perhaps a bit more exotic and exciting, but a race car nonetheless. It could have been Dale Earnhardt's Winston Cup Chevy Lumina without fenders, for all I could see. The designers had more latitude than those at NASCAR, but the concept was the same: Tune the engine, grease all the parts, and it goes fast.

But what I found was that in Indy Car racing, the entire package is the car. It is not a restrictor plate that slows it down, as in NASCAR, nor is it CART's (Championship Auto Racing Teams—the regular season sanctioning body) reduction of turbo boost over the years, which is now at embarrassingly low pressures. It is not a gear, an engine, a chassis, or a driver. It is *the package*.

The magical Indy Car. Look sharp, but don't focus too long on any one thing or you'll miss something else. If you focus on the engine, you'll miss the amazing precision of the chassis; look at the chassis too long and you'll miss the electronics that make the aerodynamic package one of the most efficient in racing; watch the engine and you miss the new suspension designs. It is not a group of components bolted together to make a car, but rather a car that, when separated, became a bunch of components. There is a difference. It was the entire thing, wrapped up in a neat ball and deposited at sixteen racetracks from coast to coast and in three countries. The marketing goes hand in hand with the mechanical engineering, and they are dependent upon one another.

A startling announcement made this clear in the summer of 1992: 1992 Formula One Grand Prix World Champion Nigel Mansell of Great Britian was quitting Formula One Grand Prix racing to come to the United States to go Indy Car racing.

In Europe, this announcement was to auto racing what Michael Jordan's retirement was to American basketball. The difference was that Jordan didn't sign to play for the Italian League.

At least that's the way it looked from overseas.

We knew differently here in the States.

Was Mansell the best? No doubt about it. Would he walk away with the title in his first year? Probably, but it wouldn't be easy. And as the season ended in October 1993, Mansell did indeed walk away with the title, becoming the first "rookie" ever to do so. But Mansell did not utterly dominate as the foreign press predicted. In fact, on American road courses, where he was expected to run away and hide, he had not a single win. All of his five wins, except the first one, in Australia, came on oval courses.

What Mansell can do with an open-wheeled car is nothing less than spectacular. But as is evident from his championship Indy Car year—when he won five races, tying Paul Tracy with five and leaving Emerson Fittipaldi with three—it was clear that there was no Williams FW14B to bail him out.

What Mansell had in 1993 was a plain-Jane Lola-Ford. The nearly bulletproof Williams-Renault of 1992—with its state-of-the-art active suspension that automatically levelled itself through corners, as well as an automatic transmission, electronic traction control, and carbon fiber bakes that stopped on a dime—was credited for the championship. As great as he is, Mansell, only needed to put his faith in the Williams designers. The car would do the rest—and it did just that, dominating the 1992 season.

But in 1993, the car that—for him—replaced the Williams, known as the Indy Car, played only a bit part in the outcome of the series. The result was as close as it was because the cars were as close as they were. What teams couldn't make up in technological advances (which, as you will find, are heavily legislated), they made up in preparation. Where the Williams had active suspension, the Indy Car has springs and shock absorbers; where the Wiliams shifted gears automatically, the Indy Car has a normal manual gearshift lever. The Indy Car weighs several hundred pounds more than the Grand Prix car and where the Formula One cars in stop on a dime, the Indy Car stops, well, let's say, on a quarter.

The often caustic, always spectacular Mansell had shown the skill and drive that he had displayed to Lotus' Colin Chapman in 1980. Moreover he showed in 1993 that with equal machinery, he could beat some of the best drivers in the world.

Credit the driver. Credit the car. Credit also the series.

Mansell's marketability overseas increased Indy Car attendance figures in the United States fivefold, and the Indy Car series truly became international. Suddenly the Grand Pix fraternity had to take a good look at itself—and apparently it didn't like what it saw, since it changed the rules and outlawed active suspension as well as several other devices. The show, the fraternity decided, was being sacrificed for the sake of the actors who starred in it.

But in Indy Car racing, if there is an edge for any team, it is in the orchestration. In 1993, the Newman Haas team had a better conductor than any other team. And it is in this orchestration that Formula One will eventually have to take a queue. The package is synchronized at all times.

Compare McLaren to Penske, and you'll find similarities, such as the depth of talent, the faith in the team, the success, and the devotion to victory. The trailers look alike, the cars share a common set of rules, and the colors are identical.

But as good as McLaren is, there always seems to be a fire that needs to be extinguished somewhere, and McLaren is probably more organized than most Formula One Grand Prix teams. Penske's people seem just a bit sharper and pay more attention to details, just a bit more, well, anal about the whole thing. Perhaps it's because the entire series is that way. Attention to details with an eye on making everything better.

In Grand Prix racing, there are driver feuds, team owner disagreements, rule-maker errors, back stabbing, and soap operas. That's before the show begins. When the race eventually, almost begrudgingly, does get started, things usually get worse. Since 1987, Formula One racing has been little more than a train derailment. The top two cars—a McLaren from 1988 until 1991 and a Williams in 1992 and 1993—just drove away from the freight cars, uncoupling themselves and allowing the remainder of the field to run uncompetitively in the open spaces.

Those of us who love Formula One still see its passion and remain committed followers, but we know that things could be better. We know that because we can see it here in the United States as it could be. Indy Car racing is still racing for racing's sake, not for the drama or the technology, but for the thrill of racing.

Indy Car racing may not be as glamorous as Formula One. After all, an airport runway at Cleveland is not comparable to the deserted streets of Monte Carlo. But the Indy Car series works.

Hopefully, this book will enlighten your view of the package. Because after all, its pragmatic approach at engineering as well as its focus as a business and a viable show are the reasons the series has been so successful.

Indy Cars. Even the name is utilitarian.

Chapter 1

An Indy Car History

A few years later and they might have been called "Detroit Cars," these open-wheeled marvels of speed and agility, America's greatest contribution to motorsport.

But in 1908 the fledgling auto industry was based in the industrial city of Indianapolis, Indiana, and thus the nickname "Indy Cars." Who could have known that Detroit would supplant it as the center of automotive creation? The automobile was a young machine, and auto racing a young sport.

Carl Fisher, a local entrepreneur, had witnessed firsthand the incredible Bennett Cup races in Europe.

A Miller 122. Probably Tommy Milton's. The lean and graceful 122 raced from 1923 to 1926, winning every race it entered in 1923 and thirty races of forty-five between 1924 and 1926. This is how it might have appeared on the board tracks of the early twenties. Ray Touriel

6

Ford's involvement in racing in 1935 produced no less than ten cars—five primary cars and five spares. The team was assembled by Preston Tucker and led by Harry Miller. Miller designed these two-speed geared front drivers with fully independent suspension for the Indy 500. The cars were indeed fast, with one of the "dream team" stable of drivers, Ted Horn, putting one of the Fords on the pole for the "35 race. Unfortunately, the effort was to lead to nowhere, as a steering joint which was located directly beside the exhaust manifold was essentially welded in one spot as the grease was burned out of it. Ray Touriel

He immediately saw the wisdom of using the captivating speed of racing as a marketing tool to increase domestic sales of the automobile. A competitive racer in his own right, Fisher decided to build an enclosed circuit somewhere in the center of Indianapolis for both racing and testing for the local manufacturers—manufacturers whose production eventually helped Indianapolis rank as the second-largest car producer in the country. Indianapolis, it seemed, was about to become home to American car building, and Fisher decided that he would be the man who brought it that distinction.

In Autumn of 1908, the idea of an enclosed circuit flourished, and plans were made to build a one-mile oval on farmland that had been used as grazing land for sheep.

The *one mile* oval.

In fact, if it hadn't been for the expansive piece of land that dwarfed the oval, it may have been just another circle track. Instead, Fisher, on a whim, took the straights and extended them until they more or less occupied all of the land. What he came up with was four corners measuring 440 yards (yd) each with two long straights of five-eighths of a mile in length and two shorter straights of one-eighth of a mile each—for a total of 2 1/2 miles. Fisher planned to eventually add a roadracing track through the infield, which would have taken up the remaining ground.

Thus was born the Indianapolis Motor Speedway. Strangely enough, its first race, on June 5, 1909, was a hot air balloon race. The balloon race was a success, but the first motor races—a series of auto and motorcycle races on August 19 of that year—were disastrous.

As it turned out, Fisher's marketing savvy was better than his designing skills, and the freshly laid crushed gravel and tar surface wore the inefficient tires horribly. Accident after accident occurred, killing several participants as well as a handful of fans. The final day of the outing was canceled and the circuit was closed. Undaunted, Fisher regrouped a month later, and the tar surface was covered with about three-and-one-half million bricks laid sideways and cemented in place. The job was completed in just over two months. The Brickyard was born.

A new set of races was announced and planned for Memorial Day and the Fourth of July in 1910. Although 40,000 had shown up for the balloon race (at least near the track, if not inside its gates), only about 4,000 showed for the Memorial Day race. With this meager a response, Fisher decided, two races was not a lucrative arrangement. More to the

This 1939 Studebaker averaged 89mph in the 1930 Indianapolis 500. It was an era now called the Golden Age of the American Race Car. (Russell Snowberger drove this car and Paul Rice was his riding mechanic.) Costs fell through the basement due to the Depression. The average cost of an engine was as much as $5,000 in 1929; in 1930 a competitive car cost as little as $2,000. Although the Depression was the impetus for rules changes, the idea of simplier cars forming a more competitive field had been broached internally within the AAA sanctioning body several seasons earlier. The sophisticated cars were making it hard for grassroots privateers to compete, and shorter entry lists began to appear, making track promoters wince as they had to pay a bigger purse with a smaller fan base due to less interest. Pennzoil

point, he could ill afford to hold the race twice a year. He decided on one big push and one big race. He opted against a 24hr event, which had proven so popular in Europe. He wanted to give the spectators a good day of racing without overdoing it. Considering the speeds of the time, that meant 500 miles of racing in 8hr. May 30, 1911, marked the birth of the Indianapolis 500.

The First Indianapolis 500

The track opened its gates for practice on May 1, and forty-four entries came to contest the event. Qualification was held Thursday through Saturday, just prior to the race, and those who managed to average 75mph through the speed traps were allowed to compete. Running numbers painted on the sides of the cars matched the order in which they entered, not the order in which they qualified, which was normal for the times.

There was one exception. The Marmon Wasp carried the number 32 out of respect for the passenger car "Model 32," which the Marmon company was currently promoting. The Marmon was an innovative little car in that unlike the rest of the field, it could carry only one person; there was no seating room for a riding mechanic. Its single seat was located amidship, and its body was narrowed, presumably to cut through the wind better.

Like most cars of the year, the Marmon used a channel-section chassis with a ladder-type frame. The notable feature of the frame was that it generally flexed and twisted so much that handling was limited to trying to keep the car under control, never mind tune it for cornering.

The Marmon had a huge 477 cubic inch (ci) engine that developed a prodigious 110 horsepower (hp)—about 10 percent higher than the rest of the field, some of which had displacements of 600ci. The six-cylinder power plant hit a top speed of 100mph.

The day before the race, driver Ray Harroun was bombarded with complaints and harangued for not having someone on board to watch for traffic. Reacting to accusations that he was the cause of a potential accident, Harroun quickly found a way to concentrate on driving and still watch his competitors by strapping a rearview mirror onto his Marmon. It was perhaps the first adjustment made to a car specifically for Indy. It may not have been the deciding factor, but Harroun won that first race.

The initial races at the Brickyard were lucrative only to the first twelve finishers; unlucky thirteen and back got nothing but oily faces. The purse was also paid only to those who finished the entire race—the whole 500 miles. The last survivors would often be on the track for hours after the winner (as well as the crowds) had gone home, racing in front of a dark, deserted grandstand.

As expected, attrition was high. So the rules were altered slightly. In 1912, with only ten finishers, Fisher found himself with extra money. The cars could not survive the contest, he determined, so he divided the money among the entrants, basing their cuts on the amount of laps run (giving a lone driver who finished only five laps the smallest payout ever at the Indy 500: $9). Joe Dawson won that second event in a National, a 491ci four-cylinder vehicle that was essentially a stripped-down production car, lapping the track at some 5mph faster than Harroun did.

It was turn-of-the-century America, and the movement of expatriation was on. According to the elite, America had nothing to offer, and a move toward embracing European values and European culture exploded on a national level, albeit not at the grassroots level. American Gordon Bennett, of Bennett Cup fame, was an American who saw the future of the United States in Europe. Indeed, as American arts, sports, and literature turned decidedly more anti-American domestically, Europeans considered US traditions curious, unusual, and interesting. Just as quickly as Americans migrated to Europe, Europeans flocked to the US to participate in the unique new pastimes—be they sport or art.

Throughout the first years of the Indy 500, drivers were considered celebrities, but it was the cars that captivated the audience. The first two races were won by American-built cars, but in the second 500, in 1912, Germany's Mercedes stole the show. Joe Dawson's American-made National, built by an Indianapolis car maker, won the 1912 race, but it was the Mercedes of Ralph DePalma had taken the lead shortly after the start, attracting the spectators' attention. DePalma's 4.5 liter (ltr) Mercedes lost a connecting rod near the end of the race, costing him the large lead he had built up. DePalma jumped out of the car to push it to the finish line and the crowd cheered. He finished eleventh, and an upstart American in a primitive race car had beaten the best. But from then on, the Indy 500 was a race that more or less showcased the foreign makes.

Foreign cars proved to be superior to the American makes. Jules Goux won in 1913 in a Peugeot, Rene Thomas drove a Delage to victory in 1914, and a Mercedes won in 1915. After the 1915 race, the rules changed, limiting engine displacement to 300ci.

Metallurgy was in its infancy. Engine builders knew nothing of alloys or heat treating, so they simply made the engines bigger and fatter to overcome the wear. Estimates of severe friction abound, indicating that engine development actually went on a reverse trend, with designers incorporating counter-productive innovations to the updated cars.

Builders saw the wisdom in making cars lighter, but they simply missed the concept of putting the engine on a diet until later years. By the end of the 500's first decade, speeds had risen from an 80mph lap average to nearly 100mph. The increases in speed came from purpose-built race cars, rather than production cars that were stripped and raced.

Internationalism had forever become a part of the Indy 500. Fisher saw to that when he actively recruited drivers from Europe in the early years. Reluctantly, American designers were forced to copy the successful designs of the European entries. Domestic car companies had failed to mount a rally, because their passenger car entries were simply not competitive in an arena of purpose-built race cars. From then on, the cars raced at Indianapolis evolved into a hybrid.

The only remaining 1941 Gulf-Miller Special. Miller's penchant for the technically superior led him to build this four wheel drive rear-engined six cylinder Indy Car. The car was quite progressive, with a supercharged engine and a focus on weight distribution. The car was hampered by a contractual necessity to use Gulf pump fuel, otherwise it might have done better. Four were built, two of which were totalled in speedway crashes, one which was lost in the garage fire of 1941. Ray Touriel

By the twenties, the Chevrolet brothers and the Duesenbergs were the only American manufacturers to continue to successfully challenge the fields of European factory teams or European-built, American-owned racers. Although the Duesenbergs continued racing passenger cars with decent success, the Chevrolet brothers had introduced their first generation of competitive purebred racing Chevys, winning the 1920 and 1921 races. And Harry Miller, a race car builder and tuner who really had no factory for building street cars, was building and racing cars. The American race car had come into its own by the mid-twenties.

By the 1924 season, Fisher had relinquished control of his track to one of his junior partners, James Al-lison, founder of Allison Diesel, and by 1927, it was sold to World War I flying ace Eddie Rickenbacker, who had created a automobile named after him following his return from the skies over Europe. The American Automobile Association (AAA), Indianapolis' sanctioning body, declared the formula for the Brick-yard based on the 3ltr Grand Prix formula. Although there had been a huge European contingent at Indy until that time, Grand Prix regulations had really never been considered.

Duesenbergs and Millers

Oddly, the Duesenbergs and the Millers were as quick as anything on the track. The 3ltr Duesie was a smaller version of the relatively faithful eight-cylin-

Mauri Rose's final appearance at the Indianapolis Motor Speedway (IMS) came in 1951. The offset roadster had not yet made an impression. By the end of the forties, Frank Kurtis had attracted attention by using a tubular frame rather than a ladder type frame with heavy side rails holding the whole car together. The Kurtis-designed car—similar to the Pennzoil Special—was slung much lower than the traditional Indy Car, giving it a lower center of gravity and a more aggressive stance—as well as a meaner look. The first roadster was driver in 1952 by Bill Vukovich, and it won the following year. Pennzoil

10

The start of a 1960 Indy Car race when the roadster dominated the field. Notice the offset driving position of the number three car on the outside front row. The offset cockpit defined the roaster in the early years. Also note the three sprint car styled cars in the field which, compared to the roadster look clumsy. The Milwaukee Mile/Russ Lake

der 300ci engine. Until now, the engine had been lubricated by an inefficient splash-type setup, but this 3ltr engine had a new pressurized lubrication system and featured a single overhead cam three-valve design (one intake and two exhaust). It inspired some of Miller's designs, and the following year a Miller won—after it was installed in a Duesenberg chassis.

The Miller straight-eight design was completed and built by Miller's two genius engineers, Leo Gossen and Fred Offenhauser, each of whom would find a special place in motor racing years later. In contrast to the relatively unsophisticated Duesenberg, the Miller was state-of-the-art for the time. It was a dual overhead cam, four-valve straight-eight, with tubular

piston rods, and performance enhanced by Miller's journeyman understanding of carburetor designing, which came from his manufacturing of carburetors for street and race cars.

In 1923, Miller was victorious in every American race of note, with Tommy Milton winning at the Brickyard. The switch to eight cylinders became almost universal. With the engine size limited, designers found that by increasing the number of cylinders, they could shorten the stroke, increase the rev limits, and increase horsepower. Both Miller and Duesenberg had experimented with twelve- and sixteen-cylinder power plants prior to the 1915 restriction on engine displacement, but found that the engine literally ate itself alive with excessive wear. The eights

This race marked the first event after the Cooper's debut at Indy. In three years the frontrunners would all be rear engined. Although the laid down engine and lowered center of gravity had changed both the look and performance of the series, the placement of the engine behind the drive in 1961 would revolutionize the series and essentially marked the end of the old era of Indy Cars and ushered in the new. The Milwaukee Mile/Russ Lake

were the right balance, and became the springboard for true development years down the road.

But if Miller's carburetors were the best for moving air and fuel into the guts of the engine under natural circumstances, Duesenberg radically changed the game in 1924 with the supercharger. The supercharger concept was certainly not new; experiments with it around 1908 had failed, and the supercharger disappeared—until it resurfaced in 1923 on a team of 2ltr Mercedes. The cars were far from spectacular, and were no faster than the atmospheric cars, but the supercharger caught the attention of American designers. The following season, the Duesenbergs were overshadowed by the normally aspirated Millers, which dominated both Indy qualifying and the race itself. The Duesenberg won anyway, due to attrition and impeccable preparation by Fred and Augie Duesenberg; and the trend toward supercharging was set. Miller took the idea and improved it. Although Duesenberg won again in 1925 and 1927, a Miller won in a shortened 1926 race and became the car to beat in 1928. Again in 1929, Miller established himself as the manufacturer to beat, winning every single race of consequence that year.

The period between wars in Europe was producing a new wave of creative talent in the arts and politics. In the racing world, where innovation, individuality, and creativity were standard operating procedures, designers stepped up development of race cars. The supercharger was seen as the ideal setup, and the AAA scrambled to keep speeds down. A 1.5ltr displacement limit on supercharged cars dropped speeds and increased the sophistication of the engineering as the top designers fought to find ways to keep the lap times up.

So even though Duesenberg had introduced a viable plan for supercharging, Miller brought the best setup to supercharging: a front-wheel-drive car. Front-wheel-drive cars dominated the tracks from Syracuse to Beverly Hills and impressed the masses, but they often didn't impress the drivers themselves. As a result, there developed two factions: those who preferred their Miller supercharged straight-eights driving the front wheels and those who wanted to race classic rear-drive cars.

But as the high-tech race builders began to appear, the high-society players suddenly dropped out of sight as October 24, 1929—Black Thursday—dropped the country into recession and subsequent depression.

The period that followed at the Brickyard was called the Junk Era, and most of the field, which was now mostly domestic garbage (cars were literally sometimes compiled of parts found in salvage yards), was American-built. The end of the depression found American machinery in a leadership role on the racetrack. In fact, the transformation from follower to leader had actually begun earlier than that. Europe had trouble simply surviving the turmoil caused during World War I. Overseas, society was turned upside down; the elite were no longer privileged, and individualism became lost in collectivism—eventually

AJ Foyt's regular race car did not arrive on time for the 1965 Milwaukee race. Foyt used his sprint car which he had competed in Springfield the previous day... and promptly won stuck it on the pole for the race. Here he leads the field to the green flag, having prepared the sprint car for the pavement by himself. He would eventually finish second to Gordon Johncock. Most cars had evolved to rear engine designs, but Foyt, as well as a few entries in the rear, showed that there was still a bit of life left in the front engine configuration. The Milwaukee Mile/Russ Lake

This photo of Mario Andretti was taken in 1966. This was Andretti's second season in Indy Cars. Although the car he is pictured with here is his sprint car (the photo was taken at Du Quoin, IL), Andretti was equally adept at guiding either type of car around the track. The days of all-around drivers has disappeared and it is odd for a driver who is an expert on the dirt to translate that ability to the pavement. It says less about the drivers than it does about the cars, which have become so technical and so idiosyncratic that it takes years to understand handling nuances of car so affected by aerodynamics. In Andretti's early career, he was the component who made the car successful, not vice versa. Dorothy Beeler, Texaco

known as nationalism, Fascism, Socialism, and finally Communism.

Racing in the Golden Age

During what is now called the Golden Age of the American Race Car, engines cost as much as $5,000 in 1929; in 1930, a competitive *car* cost as little as $2,000. Bad times forced deep changes. Supercharging, an expensive performance enhancer, was eliminated with a rule that no *four*-stroke engines could be supercharged—not banned, just effectively removed from race cars. The limit was now two valves, not four, or four valves and one carburetor barrel on any engine. Bodies, which had been streamlined in the twenties, were legislated to have two seats again; and engines were brought back to 6ltr.

The Great Depression was the impetus for the rules change, but the idea had been broached internally within the AAA several years earlier. The sophisticated cars were making it hard for grassroots privateers to compete, and the entry lists grew shorter, which in turn made track promoters wince as they had to pay a bigger purse with a smaller fan base due to less interest.

The new rules not only allowed, but actually encouraged, street-based race cars. The "run-what-you-

A 1977 "shovel nose" Dick Simon car. Following this season, car design became more of a unwitting committee decision—whatever the consensus seemed to be, the field followed. Before 1978 or 1979, designers still relied a great deal on the driver to bail them out of whatever mistakes they made in the car. By 1980, no matter how good the driver was he couldn't drive himself out of a poorly made car. The Milwaukee Mile/Russ Lake

brung" series had vigorously embraced the passenger car market. Unlike today, with cars of all shapes and sizes and engines spanning the gamut from 850cc two-cylinders to 7ltr, cars of the time were big-bodied and blessed with beefy engines. As they had done in the early-1900s, racers went to the track with street cars stripped of fenders, windshields, and running boards. They were competitive.

Very quickly, the tuners reappeared and began to attack the new formula with a zeal equal to that which they had shown years earlier. Compared to racing's first years, the thirties were a time of innovative ideas that simply needed refining. Old technology was retrofitted to the new, simpler technology, and former concepts came back—such as winning on Sunday and selling on Monday.

With the new formula based roughly on street machine performance, it was natural for street car manufacturers to return to racing. What most felt would be a death blow to racing became its help-

Danny Ongias takes the checkered flag in the 1978 Tony Bettenhausen 200 at Milwaukee. The Interscope Racing entry was a Cosworth-powered Parnelli Jones car and won more races than any other car that season. Unfortunately for Ongias—who had a reputation for bad luck—he did not win the championship. Instead, Tom Sneva won the title in 1978... without posting a single win. The following season CART would revolt against USAC and form a second series. The Milwaukee Mile/Russ Lake

ing hand: Ford, Studebaker, Hudson, and Stutz, to name a few, saw the positive media attention from racing and devoted a great deal of energy to the sport.

Factories were quick to hire the established designers. Ford smartly rescued Harry Miller from near bankruptcy. Preston Tucker, creator and namesake of the Tucker Car, convinced Ford to use the Indy 500 as a way to advertise. Ford agreed, but insisted on using Harry Miller, who fielded a five-car super-team. The guts of the car was a modified stock Ford V-8, and it even used a 1935 Ford grille. The car was extremely competitive in qualifying and might have won in

1935, had there not been a small steering design flaw that caused all of the Fords to drop out.

The 1935 race was really the last time any Millers were competitive. Miller would make a final serious run at the Brickyard in the late-thirties, but his heyday was over. And Fred Duesenberg was killed in a car crash in 1932, which effectively ended the Duesenberg reign. But two other know names returned bigger than ever: Fred Offenhauser and Leo Gossen.

The Rise of the Offy Engine

The two had worked on a 3ltr hydroplane racing four cylinder engine, a power plant that experienced

16

Tom Sneva, pictured here in his 1983 Cosworth-March Texaco Star, won the 1983 Indy 500. After two season stint as a non-championship CART event (due to USAC sanctioning) the race reappeared as a USAC sanctioned event but counting toward the CART Championship. The Milwaukee Mile/Russ Lake

something of a renaissance in the thirties in sprint car racing. The little four was simple and lightweight and worked well in the sprint cars. Offenhauser and Gossen, still working for Miller, realized the potential for the new formula and redesigned the Miller hydroplane motor. Its distinctive feature was a single block/head casting with the crankcase made as a separate piece of the engine. The engine won its first race as a rebored and restroked Miller four, but by 1935, the "Offy" had its first victory, beating Miller's Fords. Miller had dissolved his company two seasons earlier, so Offenhauser and Gossen were already on their own. In 1934, they officially opened Offenhauser Engineering. The unsophisticated and reliable Offy battled with old twenties Millers for most of the next

decade, and it took eight years before the lap record set by a Miller at Indy in 1928 (122.391mph) was eclipsed.

Superchargers had kept the compression ratios down, but the new rules sent them higher than they had ever been, and valve gear technology gave the cars more efficient breathing. It was a time of tuning and making do, and the goal was to make the race series more competitive than anyone expected.

In 1936, the Speedway was repaved and its walls were angled. This alone accounted for a huge gain in lap speeds. But more was needed, and in 1937, the Speedway sought a way to encourage overseas participation, which had pretty much been nonexistent after 1930. Acquiescing, the AAA again allowed su-

Teo Fabi leads Tom Sneva in 1983. Fabi, fresh from Formula One and a competitive winner in World Endurance Sports Cars, became the Indy Car Rookie of the year in 1983, amassing more points than any rookie ever and tallying four wins as well as the pole for the Indy 500 (in only his second Indy Car start). The record season was double what any rookie had ever accomplished. It was rather quickly eclipsed by Nigel Mansell, who came to America as reigning Formula One World Champion in 1993. The Milwaukee Mile/Russ Lake

percharging on four-stroke engines, and thus encouraged Grand Prix cars—all of which were supercharged at the time—to return to Indy. The following season, the rules paralleled the Grand Prix formula in Europe, ultimately leading to a return to the ultra-sophisticated engineering of the twenties.

The formula was based on a 4 1/2ltr formula for non-supercharged cars or 3ltr for supercharged. The rules did, in fact, attract European cars, but no European manufacturers. The Silver Arrows, the incredible Mercedes dominating Grand Prix racing at the time, did not come at all. A handful of second-hand Maseratis and Alfa-Romeos ran at Indy, eventually winning the 1939 and 1940 races at the hands of Wilbur Shaw, but essentially the formula was still American.

It was still a positive change, however, since it spurred American design changes.

Art Sparks and Joel Thorne created what was essentially a six-cylinder Offy with a few innovations.

The supercharged power plant produced more than 450hp at about 5000rpm, which broke the eight-year-old lap record. Its short stroke allowed revs to rise and in turn quickened the supercharger rotation, which pumped more air. American engineers immediately saw the advantage of higher-revving engines.

At the same time, Lou Welch, whose Ford V-8 tuning shop in Novi, Michigan, saw the advantage of using the Offy-inspired integral head/block construction, but as a V-8. The "Novi," named after his Michigan hometown, could rev nearly 8500rpm, a prodigious feat in those years. But on-track technology was overshadowed by technology on the battlefields of Europe.

The Post-War Years

The world went to war once more. The Brickyard—with only its front straight still lined with bricks while the rest of the circuit was paved with asphalt—shut down for three seasons. When it reopened, it

18

Danny Sullivan's 1988 Penske in which the popular driver won four races and set pole qualifying time nine times that season. He went on to capture the championship that year. Compared to contemporary cars, the Miller-sponsored Penske

PC-17 is dumpy and rather sluggish looking; compared to the Miller-sponsored Cosworth March in which he won the '85 Indy 500, this car looks like an arrow. Miller Brewing

was under the command of three-time Indy 500 winner Wilbur Shaw, who had convinced Tony Hulman to purchase it from Rickenbacker. With the Hulman family backing the facility, the Speedway began to prosper again in 1945, and as the country came from depression to growth, the Indianapolis Motor Speedway began growing as well. The return of the race in 1946 was met with huge success; postwar regulations were the same as before the war, but with no minimum weight.

The pre-war cars reappeared and, finally, the Mercedes Grand Prix cars found their way to the Speedway. An Italian Maserati factory team also tried to conquer the bricks. The post-war period was marked by a lack of direction. Cars as sophisticated as the V-12 Mercedes were losing because nobody could understood the car and how it should be tuned to Indy standards. At the same time, there seemed to be no perfect combination. Technological growth came mostly from chassis development. Engines had evolved to a very high stage, but the chassis and suspension failed to keep up.

Still using solid axles and leaf springs, the cars were returning to their old attitudes of the teens:

they had great power but no refined handling characteristics. Although Grand Prix cars were inherently better-handling machines than Indy Cars, they were ill-suited to Indy's unique demands. America mechanics were used to setting up cars so that they could drift into a corner, sliding all four wheels. Keeping the car stuck meant headaches that nobody really wanted to deal with. But they ultimately had to deal with it.

Miller had discovered more than ten years earlier that less unsprung weight—that is, weight not "hung" on the car, such as wheels, tires, control arms, and suspension components—meant better handling. Unsprung weight helped the wheels stay on the ground over relatively bumpy surfaces—and in the late-forties, at racing speeds, everything was bumpy, even though the Speedway had been completely repaved. By the end of the forties, racers had revolutionized the look of the Indy Car by adopting new, lightweight magnesium wheels.

In the fifties, Indy cars raced on a wide variety of tracks, including road courses and ovals, dirt tracks, paved tracks, and the Speedway at Indianapolis. The American Automobile Association (AAA) sanctioned

Veteran A. J. Foyt has retired from racing to run the team he owns. A fout-time winner of the Indy 500, the mercurial Foyt will be regarded as one of the best of all time in any series; he just happened to call Indy Cars home.

Championship series (Indy Car) racing until 1955, when it pulled out of racing completely. The United States Auto Club (USAC) was formed to sanction Championship Trail racing—where Indy Cars competed—along with Midget, Stock, and Sprint car racing. It's also noteworthy that in the fifties, Indianapolis 500 results counted in the Drivers' World Championship (Grand Prix) points race.

Although hydraulic shocks had appeared in the thirties, the explosion in shocks came with the telescopic shock introduced by Monroe Automotive Equipment Company in 1950. And by the end of the forties, Frank Kurtis had attracted attention by using a tubular frame rather than a ladder-type one with heavy side rails holding the whole car together. It was essentially the first Roadster. The car was slung much lower than the traditional Indy Car, giving it a lower center of gravity and a more aggressive stance, as well as a meaner look. The first Roadster was driven in 1952 by Bill Vukovich, and it won the following year.

As the cars got lower, builders realized that the reduction of frontal area also improved the race car's overall performance: Less wind equaled more speed. The concept was to proliferate ten years later, when designers became preoccupied with aerodynamics.

The solid front axles were replaced by independent front and rear axles, torsion bars were experimented with, and tires became wider and were now made with nylon cord which stayed cooler under racing conditions, thereby wearing better. The improved speeds brought new advances in braking. It was essentially an expansion period, and as soon as the racing fraternity got used to the suspension revolution, it had to deal with a new type of car: the Grand Prix racer.

The Innovations of the Sixties

European racing was roadracing on asphalt. American racing was basically an oval track affair, often run on dirt. But innovation became the standard operating procedure of Indy starting in the early-sixties, as race cars, like modern art, were defined by their creativity. Whereas the gains of the mid-forties to the late-fifties were made by a slow evolutionary process, the gains of the sixties and seventies came at breakneck pace.

Lightweight cars began to dominate the sport. In 1961, Cooper Cars, of Great Britain, sent Aus-

The legendary Rick Mears sports a new look after hanging up the helmet and going to work at trackside for his old boss, Roger Penske. Mears won the Indy 500 four times, and his technical knowledge and set-up expertise are legendary.

20

tralian Jack Brabham to Indy in a small, fragile-looking rear-engined Grand Prix car whose power had been enhanced somewhat to compete with the more-muscular Indy Cars. At best, the car still had a 35 percent power disadvantage. Cooper and Brabham were ridiculed, but nonetheless finished ninth and showed exceptional handling, creating interest in the design.

Dan Gurney approached Lotus' Colin Chapman in 1963 to build a rear-engined car with a very low center of gravity. The Lotus' Ford engine was set in the back of the car and was slung very low. It used efficient monocoque construction and was far lighter than its counterparts. Gurney had problems in the race, but his teammate, Jim Clark, finished second to Parnelli Jones, eventually winning an Indy Car race in the rear-engined creation at Milwaukee a few months later, and then taking victory at Indy in 1965. In 1965, in essentially a copy of the Lotus, Mario Andretti won the Indy Car national championship, marking both the first year a rear-engined car had won the championship as well as the first year a road race had been run as part of the championship since the pre-war years of the prestigious Vanderbilt Cup.

The series was still Indy Cars, and it still revolved around the Indy 500, but the cars and the disciplines needed to win a driver's championship varied from dirt to asphalt oval with some road racing. The cars were expected to take it all in stride.

By 1967, not a single car was front-engined, and within six years, dirt track races were eliminated from the schedule and engineers concentrated on developing the cars for asphalt only. The focus was still on Indy and the long, flat surfaces of the track known as the Brickyard.

At that time, the 255ci Offy was still the engine of choice, but Ford was about to become the marque to beat. The Ford factory launched an all-out assault on Indy in 1963. The Ford V-8, which was basically a Fairlane passenger car design and used pushrods and a single cam, was installed in the back of Jimmy Clark's Lotus and nearly won the race. It tried, and failed, again in 1964, but its third attempt was successful and it went on to win eighty-five races.

Using the exhaust to power a turbine for ramming air into the intake—a turbo—the old Offys had nearly 600hp, which saved them from extinction. Ford engineers followed suit, but Bobby Unser's Offy won in 1968.

Things were about to get weirder. Look back to 1961, when John Zink brought a Boeing gas turbine to Indy. Although the car completed only a few laps at the Speedway, it started a movement that would culminate in 1968 with nine gas turbine cars, the most famous being the STP Lotuses. They were eventually banned, along with the other new technology such as four-wheel-drive, which had been experimented with in the late-sixties.

Bobby Rahal is shown after winning the PPG IndyCar World Championship in 1992. In 1993, the wins—as well as simply qualifying for the main event, the Indy 500—would not be so easy.

Gone were the weird-looking engines, but here to stay were the weird-looking cars. The first wings appeared on Grand Prix race cars in 1968. They showed potential, but also proved to be dangerous as wings collapsed. By 1971, the revolution in aerodynamics had begun.

The speeds had come up. Compared to the first race in 1911, when the average lap speed had been about 80mph, by the sixties, speeds were approaching 150mph, a gain of only about 12mph per decade. That changed in the seventies. As technological advances came more quickly, speeds rocketed. Lap speeds hit 180mph in 1971, jumped to almost 196mph the next season, and reached a mind-boggling 202mph (by Tom Sneva) in 1978. Most of the changes were a result of a greater understanding of aerodynamics.

The shapes of the cars changed, going from big, bulky, front-engined Monopoly-car Roadsters to small, lightweight, aerodynamic creations—some of which were as slippery through the air as a brick.

The Offenhauser, which had dominated the circuit for so long, was eventually aced out by the Cosworth DFX, which won its first race in 1978, more or less signaling a new era of the sport. The metamorphosis was completed in the next season, with the formation of the Championship Auto Racing Teams (CART) series, founded by Pat Patrick, Roger Penske, and a handful of other renegade team owners. (For marketing purposes, the group now uses the name IndyCar. CART uses the IndyCar name and logo

New nineties contender Robby Gordon was gaining experience in off-road racing and got a taste of circuit racing when, on a lark, Roush had him test for the Roush Trans Am team. Without having previously been in the car and without being near the optimum line on the track, Gordon was one of the quickest drivers in the test. He was signed immediately and quickly ascended to Indy Cars.

Paul Tracy is another young Indy Car driver who has proved himself. Tracy once said that driving for Roger Penske as a rookie was an infinitely more difficult job than he got credit for: He was inexperienced, yet he was expected to win races. He demonstrated his talent the first year and did, indeed, win, finishing in the top three of the championship points race in 1993.

under an exclusive licensing agreement with Indianapolis Motor Speedway.) Under the new championship, the series prospered and gained more momentum than ever. Indy became not just the greatest race of a country, but of a championship. It was the most lucrative, most spectacular race in the sixteen-race season. The championship itself has come close to being as prestigious as the 500, but not quite.

In the meantime, the series was still nicknamed Indy Cars and was never really able to divorce itself from that name nor that race. Perhaps, as pundits reminded, it never should have been. In 1992, the name was changed and the series was officially named what journalists and fans had been calling it for the previous ten seasons: Indy Cars... where we begin our story.

Chapter 2

Clearing the Air: Aerodynamics

For the most part, aerodynamics in the first sixty years of the Indy Car racing was based simply on what *looked* fast. There was little in the field of aerodynamics in the early days of the sport that was scientifically quantifiable. In fact, until recently, science had little to do with how the Indy Cars plowed through a wall of air. Most of the advances made from the late-fifties to the early-eighties were the result of trial and error. It was far from an exact science. The "If it looked like a rocket ship, it probably went fast" philosophy fell short of making any true gains.

The pre-war Mercedes were some of the few cars whose design benefited from wind tunnel testing. The Germans found that most of the drag on a race car came from the wheels, which obviously couldn't be eliminated. Some teams tried to partially cover them with some success, but this was still an open-wheeled formula.

The first car to make an impact in the area of aerodynamics was the Cummins diesel which made its appearance in 1952. Cars in general were getting smaller, lighter, and more aerodynamic when Cummins came out with its sleek design, a move based more on weight control and a desire to lower the center of gravity than anything else. With its resulting low-slung body, it was more slippery, but the wheels and tires still gave the designers trouble—in terms of both wind resistance and the tires' limits of adhesion at speed, a seemingly impossible situation.

But in Texas, while working with sports cars in the early sixties, racer Jim Hall accidentally made a discovery that would change the sport. Hall renewed his involvement in racing in 1992 as an Indy Car team owner, and is still considered the father of racing aerodynamics. The accident that aided in the development makes an interesting story.

'Discovering' Aerodynamics

"What happened," Hall relates, "is that I decided to build a mid-engined Chaparral in Texas. We got the car finished, and we decided to go out and test it.

We didn't have the bodywork done, so we just ran it without bodywork. We had run them without the bodywork before and we didn't think it was that dumb an idea. Anyway, we could watch everything work. We started out pretty slow, but we found that with a little windscreen on it, we could run it pretty hard. And we did that.

"Then the bodywork got finished and we fitted it, and we found out that for some reason, we were immediately slower. That was surprising to us at the time. So I started to instrument it. I found that when I went down the high-speed straight-away—there was a slight bend in the test track—I had absolutely no grip at all. It was real obvious that we had a bad body. It was real detrimental to the car, which meant we had to fix it. The lap times when we ran the car with no body was two or three seconds faster than when we ran it with the bodywork on it! So that's how I got interested in aerodynamics. I said, 'Gee whiz, if the forces are that great on the car that it could screw up the handling of the car,' well, my first thought was to fix it.

"But then I realized I could help the car with aerodynamics. I think up until that time, people tended to think of aerodynamics as a negative. They said, 'Well, let's reduce the amount of drag or the amount of lift on the car.' Some engineer said, 'it's round on the top and flat on the bottom, so it must lift.'. So everybody said, 'Well, let's reduce the lift by reducing the drag.' It just occurred to me that I've got all that force to deal with; why don't I use it to help me? That was probably my contribution right there—that idea.

"I started changing the front of the car to change the lift. That ended up being the snowplow device on it. My first thought, to tell you the truth, was the same as everybody else's: to build a car that didn't lift. And I did that. I made myself some gauges to measure the lift. And I built a car that didn't lift at all. Then I wondered, 'Well, what do I really need now?'"

The full wings came in 1966. Hall had started putting more and more down force on the cars in

1964, and in 1965, he used a little slap wing. Each time he improved the body, his lap times dropped. Eventually, the cars had substantial download—and drag. They weren't very fast on the straight-away.

"People would pass us on the straight-away," according to Hall, "so we tried to figure a way around that. So instead of a fixed flap we put a moveable flap on it, which increased our straightway speed and gave us the same braking force and download in the corners. That was the first thing we did in 1965. What happens is that you put so much down force, the car squishes to the ground and you lose your springing. So I thought, 'Why don't we get it off the sprung mass and get it onto the unsprung weight?' So I stuck it onto the wheels. That's what we ran the first time. It was really quite a nice car. It was a good way to do it."

Wings had appeared on sports cars as early as 1964, and on Grand Prix cars by 1968. The wings tended to break, which caused some horrible acci-dents. They also looked ridiculous. Although wings in-evitably returned, moves were afoot to renew the ban on wings, or at least reduce the swept area and height so they could not work effectively.

The sanctioning body called USAC—the United States Auto Club—ruled that the highest part of the Indy Car could not be any taller than 28in. In 1969, aerodynamics were slightly behind in the United States compared to European racing, but USAC had been monitoring European developments and limited Indy Car front wings to 9in on either side of the body, without exceeding the center line of the tire.

Making Aerodynamic Advances

In 1971, the aerodynamics regulations changed to allow much more latitude. What had appeared prior to 1971 had been essentially a race car with aerodynamics that were developed more or less inde-pendently, then mated for competition. In other words, wings were almost an afterthought. The

Aerodynamics of the early years was devised around what looked fast. As designers found out forty years later, what looked fast usually wasn't. Ray Touriel

The field in 1966 from the rear. In 1966 there were almost no aerodynamic aids. The last car in this line has a mild "duck-tail", which was the precursor to the modern rear wing. Grand Prix drivers and teams would experiment with wings and air- foils in 1968 and by 1969 the wings were universal enough that USAC began restricting their size. The Milwaukee Mile/Russ Lake

1969 was the first win in what many thought would be a long string of victories at Indy for a 29-year-old Italian immigrant. Unfortunately, the "jinx" has been in force ever since and Andretti, who tops most list in "all-time" stats, with the most poles, most laps led and second most victories behind AJ Foyt., only won the famed race once in nearly thirty years of pro racing on the bricks. This car marked the first season where USAC regulated the length and width of aerodynamic aids. The devices really only addressed drag and were still not efficient in managing the air for the production of downforce. Nevertheless, they were far safer than what had evolved in Europe, which was a series of very tall, very prominently mounted and very dangerous wings. Dorothy Beeler, Texaco

USAC rules addressed this style of engineering, limiting the rear wing—or actually the car in general to a maximum height of 28 inches above the track surface; the front wing was not allowed to extend past the middle of the front tires. The rules makers had regulated the 1971 designs based on their ideas of what a car looked like. Wings that had appeared just a year earlier were massive things mounted many feet above the ground. Surely by keeping the height to a minimum and the width to a set standard, the aerodynamic craze would die out. Except

for designer Gordon Coppuck. The 1971 McLaren was designed around these new regulations. Rather than making the devices a separate part of the car, the McLaren designers made the *body itself* a part of the aero package.

The McLaren M16 used twin low-mounted nose radiators to reduce drag and allow the creation of a wedge-shaped front end. The shocks were mounted inside the bodywork, and the rear wing was designed to contribute 500-600lb to the rear wheels at speed. While most wings were previously aimed at

Mark Donohue in his 1971 McLaren M16. In 1971, USAC rules limited the rear wing—or actually the car in general—to a maximum height of 28 inches above the track surface; the front wing was not allowed to extend past the middle of the front tires. The rulesmakers had regulated the 1971 designs based on their ideas of what past Indy Cars looked like. Wings that had appeared just a year earlier were massive things mounted many feet above the ground. But rather than making the devices a separate part of the car, the McLaren design-ers made the body itself a part of the aero package. While most wings were previously aimed at redirecting air and reducing drag, the McLaren's wing was designed to reduce drag and produce down force—a revolutionary concept at Indy. Donohue and teammate Peter Revson were immediately almost 10mph faster than the previous year's fastest speeds. They were able to hit nearly 220mph on the straights, while Donohue posted the lap record of 180mph in practice. The Milwaukee Mile/Russ Lake

redirecting air and reducing drag, the McLaren's wing was designed to reduce drag and produce down force—a revolutionary concept at Indy. The front wings, which had been essentially regulated to about nine inches from the bodywork on each side of the nose (the average car in 1969 had nine inches between the side of the body work to the mid point of the tire), were now massive devices that were far more efficient than they had ever been. Yet they were within USAC's rules.

Driving McLarens, Mark Donohue and Peter Revson were immediately almost 10mph faster than the previous year's fastest speeds. They were able to hit nearly 220mph on the straights, while Donohue posted the lap record of 180mph in practice.

In 1972, with everybody beginning to experiment with wings, USAC changed the regulations again, essentially opening the way to the modern era of aerodynamics. By changing the regulations to the current maximum wing height of 32in above the

In 1972, with the success of McLaren, teams began to experiment with wings. The huge advances made by Donohue and Revson in 1971 were immediately eclipsed by a huge margin. The more astute teams (shown here leading the 1972 Milwaukee race) found that they could nearly double the weight of the car by using efficient wings and effective aerodynamics could offset weight gains. Lap speeds for Dan Gurney's Eagles went from 180mph to almost 200mph in just a year. Oddly, although overall lap times were almost 20mph higher, and the cornering speeds were nearly 15 percent faster, the straight-away speeds were down more than 10mph. Just as the designers had created down force for cornering, they had also created drag that manifested itself in slower straight-away speeds. Therein lies the compromise of the modern race car. The Milwaukee Mile/Russ Lake

ground and allowing the wing to be separated from the car, USAC officials allowed a huge area of experimentation. The advances made by Donohue and Revson in 1971 were immediately eclipsed by a huge margin.

By the following season, more astute teams found that they could nearly double the weight of the car by using efficient wings; effective aerodynamics could offset weight gains. Lap speeds for Dan Gurney's Eagles went from 180mph to almost 200mph in just a year. Oddly, the gains were also sacrifices. The overall lap times were almost 20mph higher, and the cornering speeds were nearly 15 percent faster, but the straight-away speeds were down more than 10mph. Just as the designers had created down force for cornering, they had also created drag that manifested itself in slower straight-away speeds. Therein lies the compromise of the modern race car.

In 1974, USAC once again changed the rules to combat the escalating speeds at Indy. The maximum width of the rear wings was limited to 36in, which was nearly 2ft narrower than the big wings used in 1972-1973. For a brief time, the speeds were kept down.

But while the sanctioning bodies tried to reduce the danger in one area, the designers made performance gains somewhere else. In the seventies, the buzzwords were "down force" and "aerodynamics." The man who watched one of his drivers take a Lotus-Ford to victory at Indy in 1965, the man who got close to winning Indy in a turbine-powered race car,

In 1974, USAC once again changed the rules to combat the escalating speeds at Indy. The maximum width of the rear wings was limited to 36in, which was nearly 2ft narrower than the big wings used in 1972-1973. By the end of the decade the area beneath the cars was being addressed. Aerodynamics had become the most important concern in Indy Car design. The Milwaukee Mile/Russ Lake

and the person who utterly dominated Formula One Grand Prix racing had made another breakthrough—and it was coming to Indy Cars.

The Emergence of the Lotus

Colin Chapman of Lotus had realized in the mid-seventies that if the swept wing area was reduced to keep speeds under control, and if more control could be gained by having a car fitted with these high-performance components, it was logical to find an alternative for the lost wing area.

What Chapman discovered while looking for another place to concentrate on the effects of the wind was that the entire bottom of the car had never been addressed. Here was a huge area that could help the down force of the car, and it had never been examined—at least not by anyone who raced open-wheeled cars. Jim Hall had already pioneered it and raced it in his Chaparral fan car, but it hadn't been done on an open-wheeled car.

"Really the first ground effects car was the fan

"I only built one Indy Car and that was in 1979," said Jim Hall of the legendary '79 Pennzoil Chaparral. "Al Unser, Sr., just drove away from everybody in the race until he had a transmission failure. But by the next year, that car was dominant. Johnny Rutherford drove for us and won the champi-onship and won Indy. That was the first ground effects car at Indy." Here Hall congratulates Unser on his front row qualifying effort. Deke Holgate, Pennzoil Public Relations

The Hall Chaparral was the first car to appear at Indy which was created especially for total aerodynamic efficiency. The goal in 1979 was not just more downforce, which had been the raison d'etre for designers up until that year, but for the reduction of drag. Look at the difference between the 1979

Pennzoil Chaparral and the Pennzoil Lola Indy winner of 1978. The Chaparral simply looks far cleaner. Note the fully covered engine cover and sculpted side pods in relation to Unsers' original car. Deke Holgate, Pennzoil Public Relations

car we built back in 1970—with the skirts around it and the evacuated air," Hall said. "That was the original idea. Then Colin Chapman took that idea and said, 'Well, gosh, maybe I can do that without the fan'. So he used the skirt part of it and shaped the underside of the car until he produced a low pressure under it and, bang, he had a new idea. We originated the thought, but he developed it in a good way.

"So that was already done, but it wasn't being applied at Indianapolis and I knew that was a good thing to do. I only built one Indy Car and that was in 1979. Wings were already well established. We did the first ground effects car at Indy. It was probably the quickest car in 1979. Al Unser Sr. just drove away

from everybody in the race until he had a transmission failure. But by the next year, that car was dominant. Johnny Rutherford drove for us and won the championship and won Indy. That was the first ground effects car at Indy."

Aerodynamics is still the black magic of racing. Small, subtle changes can make a slow car fast and vice versa. If a rear wing works just the opposite of a airplane's wing—producing reversed lift and thereby creating a force that drives the rear wheels into the ground—having an inverted wing beneath the car, where the contour of the car was the wing, can produce the same results.

Chapman redesigned the Lotus into what became known as "ground effects cars." The side pods housing the radiators were now tunnel areas that were sensitive to the airflow beneath the car. The front of the car had wide openings to invite air into the tunnels, which quickly narrowed as they reached the middle of the car. The air was severely restricted at one point, and then the tunnels expanded again toward the back of the car. So from about 3in of intake across the bottom of the body, the exit widened to about 12in. The expanding area created a negative air space that could be controlled by using a rear wing to push the car down onto the track. At the same time, the Branouli principle (which says that wind rushing by an object tends to pull the object into the stream of air) essentially pulled the car's bodywork toward the narrow slit of rushing air, that is, down onto the track. To get the best results from these cars, the entire underside had to be "sealed"

from lateral airflow. Skirts were developed to keep all the air that was supposed to be there in, and all unwanted air out.

In Europe, Mario Andretti won the 1978 World Championship in one of Chapman's Lotus 79s, but the handwriting was on the wall. Drivers were complaining that they had no "feel" for the cars, that a car repeatedly stuck and stuck and stuck some more, and then came unglued and uncontrollable. If a skirt were damaged, the car became utterly undriveable. The death of Gilles Villeneuve in practice for the 1982 Belgian Grand Prix signaled the end for ground effects, and soon after they were banned in Grand Prix racing.

In Indy Car racing, where the ground effects technology had been slower to develop, a curtailed ban—not a total one—was enacted, one which eliminated

Al Unser won the Indy 500, the Ontario 500 and the Pocono 500 in this car. The following season, in what was regarded as the most advanced car of its time, Unser sta on the pole for the start of the Indy 500. Unfortunately he was unsuccessful in his bid to capture his fourth Indy 500 victory (which he was

to finally accomplish in 1987) with the car. The following season Johnny Rutherford won five races including the Indy 500 and finished in the top five ten times. Deke Holgate, Pennzoil Public Relations

This ungainly looking beast was typical of the design philosophies of the day. Components were simply added in the attempt to gain a little here and there. In this photo the counterproductivity of having both the shovel nose as well as all the swept kickbacks along with a fairly good sized front wing is obvious. Also note how large the engine is, allowing the cockpit to extend higher than it need be. The Milwaukee Mile/Russ Lake

the skirts and limited the venturis beneath the cars.

Indy Car Aerodynamics Today

Indy Cars are now allowed a maximum rake in the undertray of 8in. Since there is no regulated ride height on an Indy Car, the venturi can start at the ground at the front of the car—or at the front of the side pods—and sweep backwards past the centerline of the rear wheels, opening to a maximum height of 8in. As in Formula One, skirts are illegal. Strakes, the vertical pieces that once ran from front to back and

The superspeedway set-up. Notice the limited down force on the speedway kit; actually, there is very little down force. The front wings are more stabilizers and foils than wings. The rear is almost flat. Additionally, the car is very streamlined.

managed air, have been eliminated, and the side pods are now open just before the rear wheels (the air once was channeled all the way back to the end of the car without interruption), which eliminates some of the effect of the venturi.

At top speed, contemporary cars can often produce three times the weight of the car from the down force. In fact, if it were possible to gradually move an Indy Car at speed up a banked turn, it could conceivably stick to a vertical wall or perhaps even sustain a negative slope—in other words, stick to the ceiling.

Contemporary aerodynamic devices are most easily tunable on the slower road courses. At Indianapolis, with its long, fast straight-aways, teams try to avoid sticking their cars to the track so much that they slow down. So there is a trade off. Ultimately, they want enough down force so that when they reach the corner, their cars can run flat-out.

Indy Car designers are continually building the cars smaller to reduce the frontal area and lessen the drag coefficient. The Achilles Heel of open-wheeled cars is the two brick-like blocks called tires. Designers can do quite a bit with the body, but the tires will always slow the sleek package down.

A Winston Cup car can run at nearly 230mph at Talladega, a banked track, with little or no aerodynamic aids. The Cup car's mechanics simply put a small spoiler on the rear end, and the car can post a top speed within 12mph of an Indy Car's posted top speed.

Consequently, Indy Car designers have to work extra hard. Unlike Formula One, where races are contested only on road courses, in Indy Car racing, there are two different techniques for two completely different types of racing—streets and oval tracks.

"There's more than one configuration," veteran Rick Mears says. "The speedway configuration is considerably different from the road course bodywork. We go so fast at the superspeedways now that the small wings are not the maximum amount of down force you can generate on these cars. The wings at the speedway are basically trimming devices; they are not the major down force. The major down force at the speedway is the underbody and the top body, to a certain extent. We really just use the wing to trim it, to get the mounts right.

"On the road courses, we produce a lot of down force with the wings. They [road course wings] are a lot bigger. We also optimize the underbody for higher drag and more down force. Even the radiator and

This Penske PC-21 is set up with what is basically a standard wing. Depending on the team, the amount of money teams want to spend, and how much testing they want to do, they may come up for more wing combinations than the standard three choices—or with fewer than three.

cooling system are different from the superspeedway to the road courses, trying to optimize download for the situation. Drag is not as important on the road courses."

Teams will experiment with wing sizes, depending on the track, but in general they have only a few choices for the season: a low down force wing, a standard wing, and a high down force wing. For most teams, there are three front wings for road courses and two different front speedway wings. On the rear, there are two different speedway rear wings and three rear wings for road courses. Depending on the team and the amount of money teams want to spend, and how much testing they want to do, they may come up with more or fewer wing combinations than that.

"At a road course like Elkhart Lake, for example, teams generally run a low down force wing since the straight-aways are so fast. A high down force wing would greatly reduce fuel mileage. Of course, once in the corners, the driver has to be careful since there will be less grip.

"The major difference between a road course and a speedway is your down force package," Mears says. "There are a lot of differences, whether it means with the gears or with the aerodynamics or your cambers and toe-ins and that kind of thing. You have rights and lefts [on a road course] versus all left turns only. But [look at the] aerodynamics first of the main [road course] package. You run a lot larger wings, a higher down force package, trying to accomplish as much down force in lower speed corners as you can.

"But on the speedway, you run a sustained 200mph or more and need a lot less down force, so you run a lot less wing. You want a lot less drag. And then you get into the chassis, for all your left-hand turns at an oval. Your toe-ins are a little different, and your camber is completely different. You have a negative camber on one side and a positive camber on the other, while on a road course, with right- and left-hand turns, the cambers are both the same way.

"Those are your two main changes and the rest of them, well, it's just gear ratios, spring rates, ride heights, that kind of thing."

The best any team can hope for is a good compromise.

The Difference in the Wings

So how do these wings—the speedway (oval track) and road course wings—differ? The low down force rear wing has a main plane with two other elements, or additional wing surfaces. Both lay back at a very low angle, so they have minimum down force; the standard wing has a main plane with two elements, but the two elements stand up at almost 90 degree angles.

The high down force wing—the cascade rear wing—has that same main plane, plus four other elements that stand up at 90deg angles also. The elements are used for what is called "trimming," or micro managing the wind after it flows over the main plane. Front wings are equipped with different flaps which can be added or removed and which have different angles so that teams can raise or lower the main plane. The gaps between the elements can also be raised or lowered, thereby creating a way for the air to escape and reducing the down force. To tune the wings at the track for varying weather conditions, teams will change the wickerbill, the little aluminum slat of metal atop the trailing edge of the element. When the tab is put on, more down force—and more drag—are created.

Wings are made completely of carbon fiber. Any decent designer will know how much down force the wing will produce, as well as how much down force

Kenny Bernstein's Budweiser King Lola. Note the arrow-like overall shape of the car. The frontal area has been reduced as much as possible for the car to slice through the wind. Designers are continually building cars smaller and smaller so the frontal area is reduced and the drag coefficient is minimal. The Achilles Heel of open-wheeled cars is the two brick-like blocks called tires that sit out in the wind.

Jim Hall is regarded as the father of modern aerodynamics. "I think you could run at Indianapolis with no wing at all now," Hall has said. "But the nice thing about the wing is that it's easily adjustable. The driver needs to have a trimming device that allows him an easy way to adjust the center pressure on the car so that it does things he'd like it to do on the racetrack. If you take it away it makes it difficult to do that. You can reduce the size so that the effect is almost nonexistent but I didn't think you need to eliminate it altogether."

will be produced at various speeds.

As designers continue trimming the existing layout, more aerodynamic gains will come from improving the undertray and bodywork. Designers know how the down forces help; what they attempt to do is clean up the airflow. They will clean up the body as much as possible, perhaps changing the kickback tabs that move air over the rear wheels or adjusting the area around the radiator side pods.

Even minor aerodynamic forces can completely change the inherent characteristics of a race car. For example, just a few turns on the elements, and the car can completely change its attitude on the track. Less wing gives less down force, which is wonderful at Indy, but not so great at Long Beach.

"The first year [1979] I sat on the pole in Indianapolis," Mears comments, "one of the last runs I made just before qualifying, I freed the car up just a little bit more. We were running basically wide open around the track. Any time you free the car up, you do two things. When you take the drag off the rear, you free the car up in the corner because [the] balance scrubs off less speed; plus you lose drag all the way down to the straightway, which in turn [means] you are also losing drag through the corner. So you help it all around the track, not just in the straightaways. So I took off a 1/8in wickerbill on the rear wing and I gained 3mph per lap just by freeing the car up a little bit more and by reducing drag. But the car would accept it because I didn't have [it] totally trimmed out yet. One more step could have been too much. I would've slowed down because I'd have had to lift more. It's very critical.

"You're trying to get that fine balance. You can make a change and completely unbalance the car. You can change a wing angle and it will affect the car one way. Then you can change the rake in the car, which changes the aerodynamic flow through the car and it makes the wing perform completely differently, affecting it in a different way. And then there are times when [a change] will affect it in the same way. That varies with spring rates and everything else. But it's very easy to unbalance the car aerodynamically; a 1/16in or a 1/32in wicker on the wing on one end or the other and you can change it a great deal.

"We're trying to make the car more efficient," Mears says in the final analysis. "I mean, that's the biggest thing, and we want to see more down force and less drag—or at least less drag—depending [on] what you are trying to accomplish. There might be times when you say, 'I've got to sacrifice down force. I've got too much down force, so let's just do away with some down force and get a lot less drag.'"

In fact, while in the seventies and eighties the key was to try to find extra grip, in the nineties, the idea is to reduce drag. That has also produced the biggest changes in component technology. With an increased interest in both frontal area and overall compactness, Ford and Chevy have downsized their engines to accommodate their engineers' aerodynamic concerns. As drivers speak of power, designers speak of profile. The engine is not smaller simply to reduce the frontal area, but also because it eventually can more effectively channel the bodywork lower, enabling more air to pass by the rear wing and perhaps allowing the use of a smaller wing with less drag.

Reaching Similar Aerodynamic Conclusions

One thing the unindoctrinated fan will notice is that there is not a lot of variety in appearance from

Jim Hall's latest work, and a variation of a theme: Hall and Lola. "I think anytime you do something like racing—I mean, it could be anything else—but people work toward the optimum setup... So the chunks of development that change the design are gong to be smaller," Says Hall. "Somebody will come along with a different idea and it will be a better one. That's what happens. The competition is a wonderful thing. Everything gravitates toward the best and until somebody comes along with a new idea, they all look alike for a while. When there's a new idea, everybody moves that direction."

car to car or from year to year. That's not just because in recent years the majority of the field has happened to run one car—the Lola—but because they have all arrived at the same aerodynamic conclusion.

When what would be considered the current era's rules package first came out, there were radical differences between cars, but they disappeared because, as Mears says, it's like "trying to fill up this envelope."

"We start in the middle of it, and slowly we work out to the edges and as you start filling up this envelope, everybody comes to the same conclusions and finds the most efficient way to go. Pretty soon, you're working just in filling in the corners, which are very small, to make gains. Make a rules change—a big rules change—and you can see new ideas. But today they're utilizing what's seems to be the best for this rules package.

"Today, a small change is [treated like] a big change compared to before because a big change is hard to find. Some examples are if you change one little shape at the front of the car, it affects the air all the way back. So you widen the front of the tub by a fraction of an inch, and it changes the air flow. So you have to change three or four things on down through the car, whether they be radiator inlets, tunnel shape, bodywork across the top, the kick up with the rear

tires, [or] work around the roll bar. Finding those still takes a lot of work, probably more work than the bigger changes did before."

In years past, when designers analyzed changes, the way they decided whether they'd made the right modifications was by standing there and by eyeballing them, imagining which way the air went. Obviously, today that can't be done. Today, the changes are very subtle, very minute, and their effects can't be evaluated by the human eye.

Says Mears: "Over the years, we've found out that the wind doesn't do a lot of things that you thought it did in wind tunnels, like as far as the direction of the wind what's happening around the tires. 'Is there spinning?' you know, getting a rolling bottom wind tunnel versus a stationary bottom. We found out of a lot of different things in that respect, just on what wind actually does, and in what directions it's taking at certain points on the car—where your high pressure is, where your low pressure is, and that kind of thing."

Advances today, small as they might be in comparison, take just as much effort and ingenuity and are just as difficult to come by as the major advances of the past. Designers are continually working on potential improvements, and are making gains in such areas as the suspension, where they're reposi-

"The major difference between [the setup for] a road course and a speedway is your down force package," former Penske driver Rick Mears says. On the road course "you run a lot larger wings, a higher down force package trying to accomplish as much down force in lower-speed corners as you can. Versus the speedway where you're running a sustained 200mph and better, you need a lot less down force, so you run a lot less wing."

tioning components such as the shocks, the wishbones, or the wheels themselves, for example. The goal is to try to design the car in a way where the suspension geometries continue to accommodate the air flow. Before, they worked on the car's body and they never really addressed the things that stick out on in the air all that much. Today, they're trying to make complete changes in suspension pick-up points to accommodate the air flow.

"If you change one spot," explained Mears, "You have to change three others to accomplish the same thing. And so there are different ways of doing that. Depending on what size, shape, and nose you have determines what size, and shape radiator inlets and leaning edges to the tunnels and that kind of thing as far as ground effects goes. I don't think they exhausted the rules when the made that change."

There will always be continuation and evolution. Unless somebody stumbles onto a design that no other designer knows about, major changes from here on are unlikely.

"I think they pretty much exhausted most of the

things for our rules as far as whole new concepts are concerned," says Mears. "I think if they ever make a major change in the rules package to eliminate down force, you may see some major rethinking going on and major designs changes. But until then, it's going to be more the same."

Might Designs Last Longer?

Teams that ran 1993 Lolas found that there was basically no difference between their cars and the previous year's cars. The fallout for the current teams is that they may be able to keep their cars longer before replacing them; or at least, the cars are still competitive for sale to teams with smaller budgets. Mears talks about things running in cycles, saying that the cars will remain the same for several seasons until a new and revolutionary innovation comes along. Jim Hall agrees.

"I think anytime you do something like racing, people work toward the optimum setup, so you get closer and closer, so the chunks of development that change the design are going to be smaller," Hall said. "I don't think there's any question about it. The more people who look at it—the more people who spend their time, effort, and money at it—it will be refined. But I think the cars are more optimized now—at least

Here's the front end of the 1993 Walker Motorsports car driven by Scott Goodyear. Notice the front wing design and compare it to that of the 1992 Truesports car, also shown on these pages.

Here is the 1992 Truesports chassis design. The front wings are equipped with different flaps that can be added or taken away and which have different angles so teams can raise lower the main plane. They can raise and change the gaps between the elements, thereby creating a way for the air to escape and thereby reduce the down force.

As designers continue trimming the existing layout, gains come from improving the undertray of the car as well as the bodywork. Designers know how the down forces help; what they then attempt to do is clean up the airflow. Notice the clean bodywork over which the air can flow.

The design may be right but that doesn't keep the noses out of trouble; plenty of spares are along in case of on-track encounters. Wings are made completely of carbon fiber. Designers know how much down force the wing will produce at any given speed.

until the next revolution. People seem to think they've got a good idea of where [the design] ought to be. In the sixties, we did a lot of work on the weight distribution of the parts, the radiator location, and some other things. But somebody will come along with a different idea and it will be a better one. That's what happens. The competition is a wonderful thing. Everything gravitates toward the best, and until somebody comes along with a new idea, they all look alike for a while. When there's a new idea, everybody moves [in] that direction."

The ideas on what direction the Lola car will take vary depending on who you talk to. But one thing is certain now that Indy Car racing has moved into the era where multi-million-dollar budgets dictate who drives and what they drive in any given race: Experimentation is an exercise that needs to show a high probability of success. In the past few ultra-competitive seasons, at least three very high-visibility, high-dollar teams have had to revert to what they know how to do best—racing the car. They have had to let the builders at Lola design the car. Porsche, Galles, and Rahal-Hogan Racing were all forced to give up on their own chassis and bodywork to concentrate on tuning the existing product. Bobby Rahal's failed 1993 qualifying attempt at the Indy 500 shows what can happen when a team tries to play catch up.

But racers will always be challenged to find ways to be quicker. In both drag racing and Indy Car racing, major speed gains will likely continue to be made without changing the basic technology. But where drag racing concentrates on one aspect of the car, Indy designers concentrate on another. In drag rac-

Wings are adjustable, and fine tuning can be done with small twist cranks like the one shown here. Major changes (such as changing wings between different tracks) require more work.

ing, the package is designed to accommodate the engine, but in Indy Car racing, the engine is designed to fit the package. In the future, most of the gains in Indy Car racing will still be made on the outside. For example?

"I think you could run at Indianapolis with no wing at all now," Hall says thoughtfully. "But the nice thing about the wing is that it's easily adjustable. The driver needs to have a trimming device that allows him an easy way to adjust the center pressure on the

Winglets control the wind as it leaves the main element of the front wing. "Everybody comes to the same conclusions and find the most efficient way to go," explained Rick Mears. "Pretty soon, you're working just in filling in the corners, which are very small, to make gains."

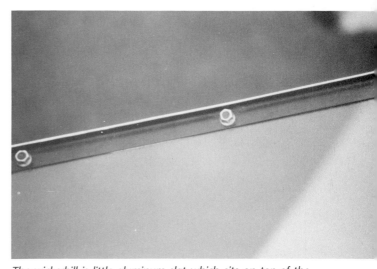

The wickerbill is little aluminum slat which sits on top of the trailing edge of the rear wing element. The larger the wickerbill a team inserts, the more down force it produces. Obviously, it also creates more drag. A change of the wickerbill is a handling adjustment sometimes made to adapt to changing weather conditions.

41

car so that it does things he'd like it to do on the race-track. If you take it away, it makes it difficult to do that. You can reduce the size so that the effect is almost nonexistent, but I don't think you need to eliminate it altogether."

"It [will] just be different," commented Mears. "As far as I'm concerned, I think they ought to run speedway wings at the mile tracks. At the rest of them, where they're kind of trying to slow the car

down, that might be the best way to do it. When I first started racing in Indy Cars, I saw guys who used to burn a set of brakes up on a car on a mile track. Today, you don't touch the brake. I used to have trouble in keeping brakes from wearing out on a car on a mile (oval). It's because you did not have the cornering speed, you didn't have the down force, you didn't have the grip for the corner. You had to slow down. I spent day after day watching guys spin

Approaches to drag and down force are the same with the rear wing (which is off the car and on end here for a set-up change) as for the front wings. Teams experiment with sizes of wings, depending on the track, but in general they have only a few choices for the season: a low-down force wing, a standard wing, and a high-down force wing. More wing combinations are possible as well for teams with the funds and test time. Here, the Mobil One team adjusts the high-down force wing.

Notice that the high-down force wing (shown standing on end here) consists of three elements. There are still fine-tuning adjustments that need to be done—especially with the triple element wing. All planes must be even and properly trimmed.

Spare wings for the rear (shown upside-down on the ground here) are at the ready. Securely attaching the wing is vitally important. A failure of the wing support is not as simple as a separation of the bodywork from the car. When a wing flies off, the car becomes completely and utterly uncontrollable.

The bodywork is slimmed down for the lowest possible drag coefficient. Drivers tuck down into the "tub" to stay out of the wind and reduce drag; only the very tops of their helmets are prone to catching any wind. Modern helmets are designed to minimize drag and keep the buffeting of the driver's head to a minimum.

Despite the tight driver compartment, the driver still needs room to shift. Notice the bump in the bodywork to accommodate the driver's hand. Anything that sticks out into the wind must be downsized and streamlined. Also notice the nicely rounded mirror and the small windscreen that channels wind around the cockpit.

The bodywork can be modified easily. Most teams come to work with a small hand drill with a set of odd-sized burrs and grinders. A few minutes of buzzwork and a new part is creat-ed. A few days of resin and cloth and an entire new set of components has been invented.

And there are infinite ways to accomplish the same goal. Notice the difference between this bodywork from Jim Hall's car and that of the Penske also shown on these pages. With so many variables in racing, there may never be a way to determine which car was a more efficient design.

and never touch the wall at a mile track. That's because they didn't have the G-loading—the side force, the cornering speed—to throw the car out.

"I was doing a photo shoot one time at Phoenix for a Pennzoil ad or whatever it was, and they wanted the speedway configuration on the car: small wings. So I was driving around the track as they were doing the shots with the small wings, and I ran the car some. And we didn't get serious about a setup other than aerodynamics, and it was pretty good. I ran it for a few laps, and I started to get comfortable with it. I mean, you have to learn to put driving back in the car. You have to throttle it. You really have to play with it. But everything was slowed down. I didn't have the G-loading. I didn't feel like I was in a rock on the end of the string."

Reinventing the Indy Car

But what if it were possible to do it over? What if a top-notch designer with an deep pockets could afford to try to re-invent the Indy Car? What would it look like?

Hall looked at the floor of his motor home, which serves as a rolling office and retreat from the nerve-racking business of racing, and then smiled broadly.

"To start over with a clean sheet of paper, you really ought to take a look at the other possibilities. I don't know what they would be at the moment."

Then, after a bit of prodding, Hall rubbed his face and grinned again. Perhaps there was something. "At the Speedway, maybe you could run a front-wheel drive car," he smiled. "It doesn't sound like the thing you'd want to do, but you ought to take a look at it to see. They've eliminated four-wheel drive cars, but you can still drive front-wheel drive cars. It's not obvious that on a speedway that would be the wrong setup. I think on a road circuit it probably is [wrong] because you need the traction control in the corners, but on a superspeedway, I guess it's a possibility. I wouldn't want to say that it's the way to go for certain, but I think you ought to

Many designers alter their bodywork—although not always with the best success. Notice the clean channels above the radiator pods. Alas, this unique detail never proved itself. Yet the trouble may have been the team, and not the design.

As the car turns to the right, the left front loads and the down force changes as the wing cocks over. Aero engineers constantly fight for a balance between a car that is too stiffly sprung and a car that can change its down force during braking or acceleration.

The difference between the high-down force package, with its triple-element rear wings (seen here), and front wing with winglets to the speedway set-up is significant in terms of af- *fect. This package would be completely inappropriate for the speedway, making the car uncompetitive.*

look at it anyway.

"If it's going to be front," he says, more animated, "I think you have the major part of the car near that area and it would be teardrop-shaped. Less drag. I think the wheels still have to stick out, don't they? I think you have to do a lot of work to see if it's worth trying something radically different from what they're running today. But I think you could

do it. I mean, today, you've got a simulation program so that you could see how it would work without actually doing it. Or you could make a model and bring it to a wind tunnel. In a few hours, you could have a big laugh and say, 'No, we're going to go back like we thought we should.'"

Or maybe not.

Chapter 3

Ever Evolving: The Chassis

Early Indy Carr chassis development consisted essentially of strengthening and lightening the frame rails. The chassis was simply a pair of beams holding the engine and supporting the body. Early cars twisted like crazy, making any tuning impossible.

The earliest competitive chassis—the Duesenbergs and the Millers—used different strategies in pursuit of the same goal. The Duesenberg used aluminum channeled frames with oak hardwood for stiffness. The Millers, as well as the rest of the field, used all-steel frames. Even by the end of World War II, chassis had progressed at a snail's pace compared with engine development. Most chassis were still these ladder-type frames with the guts of the car bolted between the two huge beams.

But by the same token, whoever thought a car could be made faster by changing the chassis? Sprint-style racing was the technique used by everyone who raced automobiles. Just get the car sideways, apply the power, and steer all four wheels out of the corner. Simple as that. Frames bent and twisted like a pair of logs lashed together with rope. The torquing of a chassis under the loads created by racing at Indy is easy to understand by our standards, but it wasn't during the early days of racing. Many efforts were made up through late forties to stiffen the torsional effects, but no breakthroughs were made. Drivers simply adjusted their driving style to the speeds.

By the late-fifties, Frank Kurtis and others began using tubes as frame rails and a network of smaller tubes to brace the main frame rails. Kurtis discovered that the space frames worked much better and that the interconnected tubing reacted to different loads and different directional forces, equalizing the chassis somewhat. The car became stiffer and much more predictable—albeit not much better-performing initially. With some persistence, sound ideas led to breakthroughs in chassis setup, and advancements in shock absorbers, wheels, and brakes resulted in even more improvements to the chassis/suspension area. During the fifties and sixties, many advances were made in chassis development for the Indy Car.

After addressing the frame, next came its relationship with the engine and drive shaft—known as the center of gravity—and where the various components were placed. The 1952 Cummins Diesel Indy Car had showed dramatically how offsetting the drive shaft could both lower the center of gravity and enhance the car's cornering ability. Eventually, the idea of offsetting the engine, the drive line, and the driver's position was embraced. Designers immediately ran with the new look, abandoning the sprint car-style layout in favor of the lower, sleeker roadster. Kurtis developed this same look on a methanol-engined car, and in 1952 is was once again a Kurtis roadster that changed the overall look of race cars. The Kurtis didn't win until 1953, but by then, the idea was catching on.

The Rear-Engined Revolution

By far, the biggest changes came in the sixties, when Jack Brabham's Cooper moved the engine to the rear, changing the handling characteristics of the car. Aerodynamics notwithstanding, the way the car took the turns was completely different. Although the Cooper was at least 150hp slower than the roadsters, it could speed though the corners better than anything at Indy. Plain and simple, the rear-engine design enhanced the car's performance.

Years earlier, Audi—or Auto-Union—had discovered that the polar moment of a front-engined, rear-wheel drive car was a main cause of uncontrollability. (To understand polar moment, imagine a pair of socks filled with sand and tied together at the top. Tossing the socks will induce an almost-perpetual spin—until they finally hit something.) Audi discovered that by putting the major components next to one another, polar moment is almost nonexistent. Unlike the larger, more powerful front-engined roadsters, the rear-engined Cooper didn't have a propen-

After disappointments in the 1993 season that included not qualifying for the Indy 500, Bobby Rahal used this 1993 Lola to resurrect his season. "The chassis is always the stiff spring as they call it, but obviously the softer the chassis and the more flexible and the more twist, the less effect suspension has," Rahal says of Indy Cars. "It just transfers loads right into the chassis rather than in the spring shock absorbers where that is suppose to go."

sity to spin, but it did tend to understeer and then snap into oversteer.

Understeer, or push, is the tendency of a car to travel toward the outside of a circle. The driver is constantly trying to keep the car turning in while it is constantly trying to travel outward. Most street cars are engineered with deliberately built-in understeer. The natural reaction of a driver on the road who has exceeded the limits of the car enough to have found the spot where it understeers is to continue steering in the desired direction. That won't work, and eventually, the driver will have to slow down—which is exactly what racers don't want to do. Oversteer, or being "loose," is when the front wheels stick to the pavement better than the rear wheels, meaning the rear end is always trying to slide or spin the car. So, understeer scrubs off speed, but oversteer, which is more desirable, creates the potential for an uncontrollable spin. Anything that could help stabilize the chassis and make it more neutral was going to improve the performance of the car dramatically. The rear engine eliminated chronic understeer and made oversteer more predictable and manageable. With the new design, the car handled like a dream, giving it a neutral handling characteristic through the corners. What drivers want more than anything is a neutral car, where the only bias is the one they add to it through steering or throttle.

With the engine behind the driver's head, the entire front end could be reworked. Tube frames, which were so great for cradling the engine, now had no real job in a rear-engined car. Sure, they were retained to cradle the engine in the rear, but it was the need to re-work the front end that changed the chassis forever. In fact, there is a good argument for the fact that for the sixties the new rear-engined cars built in the United States were still simply rear-engined roadsters, since they did not quickly embrace the new monocoque that the British were using.

Taking a queue from the airplane industry, British designers began using a structure that used the skin of the body itself to stress the frame. In other words, the typical race car used a frame over which the sheet metal body panels were bolted—the panels *were* the frame. Box-like structures formed bulkhead-type areas that pulled the skin taut—like a fence post keeps a fence straight and strong. Twisting was kept to a minimum, and weight was greatly reduced.

The 1971 McLaren showed that a longer wheelbase could enhance handling by slightly redistributing the weight. Moving the driver forward nearly a foot and placing the fuel tank directly behind him helped the weight distribution as the fuel load lightened while the race progressed. This also changed the car's appearance from that of a coke bottle to that of a wedge. Suddenly, bump steer, scrub radius, and polar moments became everyday words.

Oddly, after the engine was moved to the rear, the biggest change in chassis development came from the engine itself. Cradling the engine between two main pieces of tubing or frame pieces was the only way anyone had ever placed the chassis in a race car. Thinking logically, how could you do anything else? But race engineers never think rationally, thank goodness, and what evolved was the Cosworth.

The Historic Cosworth and Carbon Fiber

The Cosworth was a Ford-sponsored project created by Mike Costin and Keith Duckworth. This state-of-the-art racing engine first appeared at the Dutch Grand Prix in a Lotus in 1967, and at the time was called a DFV. Shortly thereafter, it found its way to Indy Car racing as a DFX turbo. The Cosworth's importance as an engine will be duly addressed in the

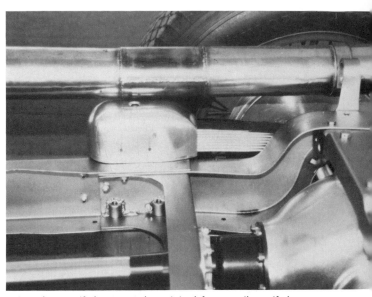

It is unknown if these are the original frame rails or if they have been replaced. Frames like these were often made with thinner gage sheet metal and strengthened with wood beams. In that way, the frames were lighter, easier to work with and nearly as strong. Ray Touriel

By the mid sixties the field had universally adopted the rear engine design inspired by the Cooper and later improved by Lotus. But the for most, the basic car remained the same, with the old tube frame cradling the engine and transmission. The cars were often just old roadsters with the engine behind the

driver. By 1966, when this photo was taken, monocoque construction was to become more and more widespread. Monocoque was the first step toward stressing the engine as a part of the chassis itself. The Milwaukee Mile/Russ Lake

49

A side view of the Lola that helped Rahal salvage forth place in championship points during the 1993 season. The inability to shake out the bugs in the Rahal/Hogan chassis more quickly demonstrated how much development time and money goes into Indy Cars.

next chapter, but it needs to be mentioned here because of its unique characteristics as an intentionally designed rigid component. That means the engine could be bolted directly to the cockpit of the race car and the wheels could literally be hung right off the engine—or the gearbox at any rate. The engine, then, *was* the car. It was not a component that could be separated from the overall handling of the car. It was the handling. It was the car.

From that point on, the overall design was firmly established, and set in stone. The adjustments ever since have been evolutionary, not revolutionary, de-

Bobby Rahal started the 1993 season in this car with its Rahal/Hogan chassis. The team had a dismal year in 1993 trying to produce its own chassis, but Rahal's teammate, Mike Groff, managed to use an updated Truesports chassis to score points in three of four starts.

A side view of the 1993 Rahal/Hogan car, which was essentially a converted Truesports chassis. The earlier Truesports cars and the 1993 Rahal/Hogan attempt were playing catch-up in a fast-paced racing game. Those failed efforts showed that in IndyCar racing, a car has to be equal before it can exceed.

One of the Penske's configurations. Note the small radiator inlets. The danger with such a design is that if the weather gets too hot, the car tends to overheat. Compare these small inlets to those of other cars seen throughout this book.

Penske's genius designer, Nigel Bennett, puts Penske's package together. Bennett helps extend Penske's sterling record as a car builder and team owner. Penske cars have competed and won in four decades.

sign-wise. But in the early-eighties, via the Hercules Composite Company, an American company the McLaren Grand Prix team had commissioned to do development work, introduced a new material that inevitably changed the way things were done.

McLaren had brought the Hercules Composite Company into racing in 1983, and the result was the eventual perpetuation of carbon fiber as a material out of which to make race cars. Carbon fiber is a high-tech-looking material, dark in color, that looks like fiberglass. Closer inspection, however, reveals that the finished unpainted product has a weave to it, like that of unpainted fiberglass. But where fiberglass is white, or beige from the resin and nylon cloth, the carbon makes the carbon fiber material gray or black.

Using carbon fiber is like bonding a durable mineral to a resin—at 80 percent the weight of other materials. It forms a very high-strength, very lightweight material. But it is a lengthy process. Excluding the engineering time to produce the drawings, it takes four or five people about ten weeks to make a master buck—a scale model—the mold, and the finished item. That's for the *first* one. After that, one could be produced every three weeks. The mold is carbon fiber itself, or wood, and it is created exactly like fiberglass.

The generic meaning of the word "composite" is a make-up of a series of materials that form a single product. The composite carbon fiber has many advantages, especially its light weight (it is lighter than conventional honeycombs), and more importantly, its ability to conform to any given shape (including very complex curves). With carbon fiber, you can make a chassis that has complex curves in it, while with aluminum, that's far more difficult.

A bulkhead can consist of three or four different weaves of carbon fiber. It might have an aluminum between layers of carbon fiber, or it might have a Nomex honeycomb sandwich. Many combinations are possible, depending on the applications, desired strength, and intended load.

The chassis of a modern Indy Car itself is usually a sandwich of materials. The sheet aluminum with honeycomb aluminum of ten years ago has been replaced with carbon fiber and a very thin aluminum or Nomex paper honeycomb.

Composite materials have been around for awhile, but their only consumer application had been in sporting equipment, such as golf clubs and tennis racquets. That soon changed, and all Indy Cars are now made of composites. The evolution and execution of the fabrication for racing very closely follows—and then accelerates—developments in military aviation.

Visualizing Carbon Fiber

So again, to visualize carbon fiber, think of a piece of fiberglass; imagine a piece of it 1/8in thick in your hand and imagine all the pieces of broken weaving sticking out. It looks and feels the same as fiberglass. The difference is that it is stronger than aluminum. That small piece of material, you'll find, is almost indestructible. It will not break unless you hit it with a hard hammer blow. When it finally does break it will shatter.

And as it continues to be developed, it is much more resilient. For example, an 1982 March Indy Car, which was all aluminum honeycomb, had a thickness of around 10,000 or 15,000lb per degree of twist. The same basic tub is now imbued with 40,000-60,000lb per degree. A more complete design, as well as the use of composite materials has changed the Indy Car into a safer and more predicable entity. "There is no movement now. It feels hard, very, very hard," says Indy Car Champion Bobby Rahal.

So not only is the strength as good as or better than aluminum, but the material absorbs the shock of an impact throughout its entire structure, essentially absorbing it uniformly rather than bending in certain spots. So it's stronger, safer, and offers weight savings for drivers.

As carbon fiber became more common in the Indy Car world, the fundamentals of design were applied and the product—as well as the way it is applied—has progressed quickly. Rahal, whose Rahal-Hogan Racing had a dismal year in 1993 trying to produce his own chassis (and who eventually gave up and bought a Lola), watched the process from both an owner's and engineer's point of view. He believes things have changed since carbon fiber was first introduced.

"The product is better," Rahal says. "Your consistency is probably better now than it was. It's man-made, and the composite cloth is laid up a certain way. I mean, it's very precise, specific measurements go into it, and I don't know if that was quite the case before. The speeds have come [up] in Indy Car racing, not from higher horsepower but from aerodynamically more efficient cars and structurally more efficient cars. The cars are much stiffer—and much safer, I might add—than the honeycomb aluminum car.

"The chassis is always the stiff spring as they call it, but obviously the softer and more flexible the chassis, the more twist, and the less effect the suspension has. It just transfers loads right into the chassis, rather than in the spring shock absorbers where that is supposed to go.

"In Formula One in some cases, the exterior, the body, is separate from the actual chassis. In others, it isn't. In Indy Car racing, what you see from the front of a Lola on back, exclusive of the side pods, is the actual chassis. With our car, it's done very similar to the McLaren, where the actual chassis is hidden by the actual bodywork. So we think it's better our way because you can change aerodynamics without structurally changing the monocoque. And we have a little more latitude for what you want to do."

As of 1993, nobody was making a complete carbon fiber car in Indy Car racing. Lola used a design that was half aluminum honeycomb bonded to the composite shell—really a two-piece monocoque. The goal was one of having a one-piece, all-carbon fiber Indy Car chassis. As the logic goes, any time you have a split, the car is only as strong as the bond holding that split together.

Take all the gearshift levers out, and the tub itself would probably weigh less than 100lb. It's safe

Made in the USA, as was this 1992 Truesports effort (which Bobby Rahal purchased later that same year), certainly does not ensure success. Indy Cars and their carbon fiber have come a long way since the technique was first introduced. "The product is better," Rahal says. "Your consistency is probably better now than it was. it's man-made and the composite cloth is laid up a certain way. I mean it's very precise, and specific measurements go into it, where I don't know if that was quite the case before. The higher speeds have come in Indy Car racing not from higher horsepower but from aerodynamically more efficient cars and structurally more efficient cars."

The chassis is formed mostly of carbon fiber, but some parts are still made from a honeycomb aluminum material. The carbon fiber is super-strong and has a weight-saving advantage as well. "They are much stiffer—and much safer, I might add—than the honeycomb aluminum car," said Bobby Rahal.

enough to take a severe impact. But if it hits the wall, turns around and spins, and hits the wall again, how does its ability to withstand the second impact compare to that of aluminum?

Engineer Steve Horne explains. "I personally think it has, depending on the design, very good secondary impact capabilities. Some other engineers said 'no, it doesn't, it should be aluminum,' but that's an argument that's been ongoing.

"I think the emphasis on the way it's engineered, the way it's put together, what materials are used, what honeycomb is in there, the number of bulkheads that might be in the car all this depends a lot on what will happen in a crash. I guess what I'm saying is don't [use] classified composite[s] in something that will not withstand secondary impacts. There's a lot more to it. It depends a lot on the engineering and the structure."

Seeking Tubular Strength for the Chassis

"Theoretically the stiffest form is a tube," adds Rahal, "because the load is equally imbued all around the circle, and that's one piece. The minute you start cutting it or something else, then you began to weaken it. Of course, in a race car, you have to have a way of putting the driver in. But you can minimize that and retain as much of the one-piece tube as possible. Then it's not going to be that much stiffer."

But there are varying opinions as to how that tube should be constructed. For a while, the trend has

been to make cars taller—at least in the smaller, more liberally legislated Formula Atlantic and Formula Ford series. Formula One cars seemed to espouse the taller-is-better design, but recently those cars have returned to their old shape.

Since there had been hardly any competition for Lola in Indy Car racing, the cars have stayed basically the same. In fact, in 1993, some teams said they could find no differences between a 1992 chassis and a 1993 chassis. That will inevitably change as designers use their seemingly limitless imaginations more and more.

"I think it's evolving in terms of the complexity of the weave," Horne says. Like, the types of resins that are being used are continually being improved. I don't see major improvements in construction techniques. I think it's still not an evolutionary process, but it's certainly not radical, like it was five years ago. The biggest change I see now is the use of metal matrix components. What I mean by that is that instead of, say, the suspension being steel, it would be a composite material in its own right."

As it continues improving, the Indy Car design will take a different tack from that of the Formula One car. Recall the difference between a ground effects car and a Formula One flat-bottom car: an Indy Car has under-chassis tunnels that need to be created as efficiently as possible; Formula One cars have only diffusers behind the rear wheels and are considerably more bottle-shaped than Indy Cars. The shape of each style race car also can dictate whether the designers use a V-12, V-10, or V-8, or even the degree of the angle in the "V" itself.

The Ilmor Chevy C engine has an 80 degree angle; the Chevy A had a 90 degree angle. Aerodynamically, the reason the Indy Car engines have become narrower and narrower is to make the front of the car thinner, thus improving the silhouette of the car—the frontal area of the car—as much as possible so it's aerodynamically more efficient.

"First of all, aerodynamics are probably still the major overriding factor in Indy Car racing," Horne explains. "You can have everything else right, but if the aerodynamics are wrong, you are in big trouble. So a lot of emphasis is put on aerodynamics. The tub or the carbon fiber chassis itself is constructed to optimize that idea. Now, do you hang things off it? To a certain degree, you do; to a certain degree, it's integral in [the] design. The front wings, for example, are [an] integral part of the nosebox of a car—the crash structure so to speak. But it bolts on and off."

"When something is designed," Rahal says in the final analysis, "you must take into account the discipline that it's being used for and how you'll enhance that. Chassis and aerodynamics are inseparably linked. There is no question about it."

Chapter 4

The Power to Fly: The Engines

Perhaps the strangest component of an Indy Car—the most enigmatic part of it—is the engine itself. In most other forms of racing, the engine is the most important aspect of the car, but in Indy Cars, it is simply another facet of the package. So much so, in fact, that the engine manufacturers don't allow the teams using the engine to do any tuning or "tweaking." All tuning of the power plants is done exclusively by Ford or Ilmor, depending on who produced the engine.

Which engine a team runs certainly makes a difference, but designers will attribute every gain in horsepower to the efficiency of the chassis and aerodynamic setup. But unlike, say, drag racing, where the mechanics are preoccupied with engine performance to the point where they tear the engine down and rebuild it up to four times a day, Indy Car engineers have little latitude with the adjustments they are allowed to make. They don't know everything about how the engine works, and they don't really need to find out.

"For us, the engine is just a big spacer in the middle of the car," says Randy Bain, a mechanic who worked for several years with Galles Racing. "If it works, fine. If it doesn't, well, we'll just get another spacer."

Comparing Indy Cars to, say, dragsters, is an extreme example: a dragster is basically an engine that is adjusted to go down the racetrack as quickly as possible by means of a chassis, and the chassis simply facilitates the engine. In Indy Car racing, the car itself—the chassis and shape of the body, to be exact—is adjusted to be moved around the track more quickly by the power plant. The engine is almost a given at this point, and anything the team does to change the car helps the engine move the car more efficiently. Gains in performance ultimately come from the peripheral adjustments.

Enhancing the Entire Package

Indeed, the major breakthrough on the 800-850hp Indy engine came from an engine design that

was not so much famous for its ability to provide power—which, as it turned out, was fairly prodigious—but for its ability to enhance the overall package. That was the Cosworth engine, which made its debut behind the helmet of Jimmy Clark's Lotus at the sand-swept circuit of Zandvoort, Holland, in 1967. It was revolutionary as a design because it was not just a piece of equipment that was inserted into the car that made it go. It was a part of the car—that equipment was *bolted to*—that helped it go.

In other words, the Cosworth's initial success was due to its design as a part of the frame. The cockpit ended in a flat butt area just behind the driver's seat, and the engine was actually bolted directly onto the back of the cockpit. It not only powered the car, it became a part of the frame, part of the car itself. And the transmission and wheels were bolted directly onto the back of the engine. No tubing cradled it; it existed as a separate component with its own structural integrity as a part of the body, as well as powering the car. Ford started a revolution, forcing engine manufacturers from that point on to concentrate on more than simply horsepower. For the first time, with the Cosworth, designers thought about the entire conglomeration.

Although the technology has evolved substantially, the idea, then as now, was sound: the engine was as good as it was because of its strength as a sum of the parts that made up the contemporary race car. At the time, there were no alternatives; it was a battle of the haves and the have-nots. Those with the new technology won the lion's share of the races.

Michael Kranefuss, who until 1993 was director of Ford's Worldwide Racing Division, said, "I think the reasons for the success of the V-8 in 1992 were basically the same as they were for the V-8 in 1967: the absence of anything else.

"There were not really any purpose-built engines around prior to the Chevy Ilmor and prior to the DFV," he says. "We started winning with the team Lotus, and we then made the engines available to al-

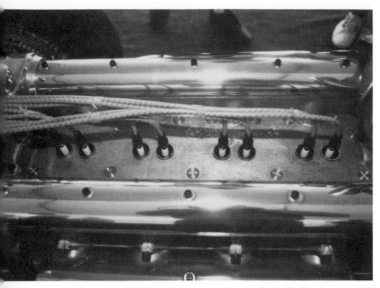

The Miller "91" engine, an in-line eight cylinder 90.2ci 285 horsepower supercharged powerplant. The 91 was super-charged and had a hemi-head design—very progressive for its time. The 91 is far simpler looking than its less powerful, larger counterparts, the 182 and the 121. The 91 won the 1926 Indy 500 with Frank Lockhart at the wheel. This one is non su-percharged, with dual carbs, mounted on the right side of the engine. Deke Holgate, Pennzoil Public Relations

Offenhauser engine number 22, was probably built sometime in 1932. Leo Goossen and Fred Offenhauser laid out plans to convert the 200ci Miller four cylinder marine engine into a competitive Indy Car engine. By 1936 the engine had evolved into a two valve hemi; then, following the sale of Offenhauser Engineering to Meyer & Drake Engineering in 1946, the en-gine was lightened; in 1965 it was downsized to 170ci— bringing the choices of Offys to two—the 255 and the smaller supercharged 170; in 1978, the Offy won its last race. In '79 the Drake shop closed. Ray Touriel

The Saga of the Turbine Engine

In every category of motorsports and in any major motor racing series, innovations from time to time can com-pletely change the look and feel of the championship. In some instances in Indy Car racing—such as Cooper's tiny, rear-engined approach in 1961, or Ford's stressed-chassis DFV powerplant in 1967—the innovations help the series move forward for the betterment of racing. Perhaps those changes occurred so quickly and with such a universal agreement that there was no alterna-tive for the field other than to adopt the new technology. Keeping up with the Joneses, so to speak.

In 1967, one Jones—Parnelli—was particularly dif-ficult to keep up with, and his experience became one of the most colorful and talked-about in Indy Car history. The story centers around the turbine engine and Jones' boss, Andy Granatelli, the man who pushed for the tur-bine's acceptance. Granatelli was deemed to have tak-en the sport in a direction that was, well, unsportsman-like. Basically, he was accused of making the turbine engine competitive.

The gas turbine had actually appeared on the Indy Car circuit in the hands of Dan Gurney and John Zink in 1962—but it was uncompetitive, at best. In 1966, how-ever, Jack Adams tried it again. Though USAC said it was unsafe and initially disqualified the engine, Granatelli, who was struggling with his unwieldy Novi-powered Ferguson, seized the idea.

Although USAC officials didn't like the idea of tur-bines on the bricks at The Speedway (even though up until 1966 turbines had never even been mentioned in the rule book), they were not actually too concerned with the phenomenon; they certainly couldn't imagine that it would nearly revolutionize the series.

Yet the turbine cars created a great deal of interest. Not only were they interesting from an engineering as-pect, they sounded absolutely awesome. The whine—and eventual scream—of the turbine thrilled crowds. USAC officials liked the concept—or at least the novel-ty—of the powerplants, but certainly didn't want them to become a common alternative to the tried-and-true pis-ton engine. To be on the safe side, USAC reduced the legal air intake area for the turbine engines.

The gas turbine engine at Indy worked by com-pressing air through a series of fans and impellers which sped the airflow into an area of decreasing size. The air was then mixed with fuel and ignited to produce a very hot, high-pressure flame. This generated power that was transferred to the wheels, and at the same time turned the compressor at the front of the engine to com-press more air. Once lit, the turbine continued running until the fuel supply was shut off. A tremendous amount of air was utilized in the process. By simultaneously adding air and fuel, the engine produced more power. Both, it was thought, were needed to increase speed on the track.

The turbine offered a few things that the piston en-gine did not: First, its fuel economy was superior be-cause its burn rate was so high. A higher temperature allowed more adjustment—in other words, less fuel—for time spent cornering, yet it provided better power on the straights. Alcohol, by comparison, is a fuel that burns at a relatively low temperature and needs constant flow. Another advantage of the turbine engine was that it was relatively light. Although ungainly in size, it still weighed less than a piston engine. Lastly, it didn't need a clutch or transmission; the power produced at the wheels rose as the engine's power was moderated. But the power could be instantaneous.

USAC took a look at the Adams car in 1966 and found that its GE engine had an intake area of about 32 square inches (sq-in). Adams' car was uncompetitive with that intake, so the arbitrary number of 25sq-in was used to effectively limit future entries—which they doubted would appear anyway.

Granatelli, however, had found a Pratt & Whitney helicopter engine with an air intake of about 22sq-in, which coincidentally fit within USAC's new regulations. It had the equivalent of about 600hp and weighed just over 250lb. Putting the engine into the area of the Ferguson chassis where the Novi was located was ridiculous, but the idea to put the power to the ground via the Ferguson's four-wheel-drive was sound. Granatelli applied the technology to the special STP-sponsored car.

The car's design was truly unique: It was built with a single aluminum "spine" down the center of the car, and to the left of the spine was the engine. The driver sat on the right side of the car. The torque was split to all four wheels.

The car, driven by Jones at the 1967 Indy 500, only qualified on the second row, and it didn't look as if it were going to be competitive in the race. But when the green flag dropped for the start it became obvious that Jones had been sandbagging. Jones passed every car ahead of him on the first lap and just drove away from the field. On the 197th lap, however, less than 10 miles from victory, a $5 bearing seized and the race was bequeathed to A.J. Foyt.

Although USAC reduced the turbine's legal intake area to just under 16sq-in, nine turbine cars appeared in 1968 (although most were never raced). Granatelli, who actually sued USAC over the rules change (he lost the suit), altered the configuration of the STP cars so the engine was centrally located behind the drivers. The cars were prepared so that the engines were always supplying at least 80 percent of the available torque. Because a turbine engine's power is generated exponentially, running at 80 percent throttle only produced about half the power that was available at full throttle. It helped make the cars fast on the track, but it changed the drivers' driving style; they were obliged to blast down the straight, get on the brakes hard and basically coast through the corner as the engine continued supplying 80 percent power, then blast off down the straight again.

No matter what the driver had to do, the cars were the fastest on the track in 1968. Mated with bigger tires and better aerodynamics than in 1967, they looked unbeatable. Joe Leonard set a track record at Indy with a 171.95 mph speed to sit on the pole for the start of the 1968 Indy 500. Again, however, the turbine cars were relegated to a footnote in history as two of the three dominant STP cars dropped out with fuel problems and the last, driven by Graham Hill, hit the wall.

Assailed by vocal condemnation by the piston engine contingent, USAC was forced to finally seriously restrict the turbine engine. For the 1969 season, turbine intake was limited to 12sq-in. Granatelli, who had to dig deep into his sponsor's pockets to modify the existing Pratt & Whitney engine in 1968, was unable to rise to the challenge. With the reduction in intake, the cars were effectively neutered. The turbine engine era faded and died. But not before fascinating the ranks of race fans and engineers alike.

most anybody. And over the years in Formula One— with the exception of Ferrari—everybody was using that engine. It also then saw its way into other forms of racing—sports car racing and so forth."

In fact, the Cosworth came to Indy Car racing as a re-configured, normally aspirated—in other words, carbureted—engine. It was converted because of its contribution as an overall performance enhancer.

"A couple of companies over here (in the United States) were racing the Offy," according to Ian Bisco, vice-president and general manager of Cosworth Inc. in the United States, "and they looked at the Cosworth and said, 'Well, if we destroked it and put a turbocharger on it, I think we can make this engine quite competitive.' There were a couple of companies— McLaren and Parnelli Jones—who did that. Cosworth themselves saw the potential with this package and made their own specifications of the engines."

So the Cosworth engine was—and *is*—important. And it was probably more powerful than anything else available at the time, but, again, its success was

Here an early Offy sits in a garden variety midget popular around 1940. Ray Touriel

This hand pump—likely an oil pump—manually moved the lubricant to the top of the engine when the engine was hot and needed the oil most. The splash lubrication did little to keep the engine lubed and cooled. Ray Touriel

based on its role in the overall package. And as we will see later in this chapter, the strategy hasn't changed all that much; the overall formula for success is still based on the ability of the engine to shrink in size, weight, and overall dimensions. Power gains from the engine are expected, but the other gains that give the overall package—the race car in general—any edge are essential for the race car to be ahead of the competition.

The Ford Indy Car engine was certainly the most modern power plant when it came out in 1991. But Chevrolet, which had seen a boom in success in Indy Car racing since the Chevy Ilmor A engine first won a race in Long Beach in 1987, scrambled to keep pace

A magneto supplied the power to make a spark—usually they were high quality units like those found on aircraft of the day. Both Miller and Duesenberg would experiment with battery powered ignition rather than gear driven magneto units. Ray Touriel

with the design changes. The package Ford brought to the paddock was smaller, lighter, and more compact. As Honda and Toyota complete their transitions to Indy Cars, they will continue adjusting the engine dimensions to mirror those of the Ford engine. Regulations completely eliminate the possibility of the engines shrinking anymore. And cost, as we will find out soon, is a major consideration in design.

Hands Off Modern Engines

So power, although critical, is not the *raison-d'e-tre* of Indy Car racing. At the same time, engine designers do everything possible to keep the design secret, which means that most team members haven't got a clue about what goes on below the cam covers. The secrets, which seem to be well kept among everyone *except* competing engine designers, are sequestered behind a mass of valve covers and plenums.

"Not only do we not [fix the engine]," says Gary Armentrout, "we're not *allowed* to do that. Under the lease program, nobody really owns their own engines. Chevy and Ford say, 'You don't take anything apart unless we have a person there.' I have had occasion to take valve covers off because we've broken a

Miller Type-H updraft carbs. The success of Miller's carburetors prompted Miller to branch out into other area of design, ultimately becoming the first racing entrepreneur. The Type-H was used by a majority of teams from the early teen into the twenties. The barrel valve revolved and uncovered a series of jets, richening the air/fuel mixture as up to six jets were uncovered. Ray Touriel

drive to the fuel pump or something like that, but you don't do any of that unless there's a designated person there.

"It's pretty much completely out of the hands of the mechanics. We can try to get the boost tuned up for optimum power. We can tell the driver to adjust his fuel control, but aside from that, that's it. You check the engine to make sure you're getting full throttle and that's all there is."

There were really only two engines in the 1993 season, only two engines that had a chance to take the championship, and on any given race weekend, the odds-on favorite were teams that used one of those two power plants—either the Ilmor engine—originally called the Chevrolet A, B, or C engine—or the Ford Cosworth XB engine. In 1993, an average engine from either leased for about $150,000 a year.

Engines are never rebuilt at the track. They are simply separated from the car, put under plastic tarps, and shipped back to be torn down, rebuilt, and re-sealed. The average teardown is done at about 500-mile intervals, and the average rebuild costs $40,000.

In any race engine, the goal is to continue development. Without the unlimited budgets of Formula One, Indy Car teams purchase or lease engines. The more the designers put into development, the more expensive the engines become. If teams want more power, they have to rebuild them faster. So instead of being able to run them 400 or 500 miles, they might have to rebuild them every 300 miles. That's every road race—obviously an enormous amount of money in anybody's budget.

So it's not really a question of the what you can get technically out of the engine, or what the true potential is; the full potential is never found. The search for an advantage never stops. Engineers will try several things with five different approaches in the hopes that perhaps one will work. For instance, the pneumatic valvetrain that was developed for Formula One would be much more reliable because it has fewer moveable and breakable parts, but the cost added to the engine would be prohibitive. Only the wealthiest teams would be able to develop the technology—and they would certainly have a major power advantage.

Louie Meyer raced this run-what-you-brung Bowes Seal Fast car to two second place finishes in 1940 and 1941. The car was a straight eight (actually, two Offy fours sealed together) with a supercharger. It raced another dozen year or so in different configuration after Meyer was finished with it. Ray Touriel

Bobby Unser in 1976 in the Bob Fletcher owned Drake-Offenhauser Eagle. Unser won in the Offy-Eagle twice in 1976. eighteen months and five wins later the Offenhauser would win its final race at the hands of Gordon Johncock and his Wildcat chassis, ending a forty-plus year run by the venerable Offenhauser engine. The Milwaukee Mile/Russ Lake

CART has made the decision not to allow that technology, and that helped the circuit field competitive grids at each race.

So, it's a question of how far the technology *should* be pushed. What effect does it have on the cost of the pieces and what effect would it have eventually on the competitive nature of the entire Indy Car series? We have seen that Formula One's approach has resulted in two or three teams sharing the glory and maybe five or ten laps of good racing at an event—before the eventual winner takes off into the sunset.

Anyone with deep pockets can develop an engine from scratch. But to what extent will the manufacturer be in the position to produce enough race engines to go racing? With the decision to produce engines must also come the commitment to service those engines. Although rules changes, recent regulations compel engine manufacturers to supply motors to at least two teams and three cars. Even then, past experience is a prerequisite. That's the major reason that both the Chevy A and the Ford XB were successful in their first years. Other companies, including Porsche and Alfa Romeo, struggled during their tenure in Indy Car racing, and each ultimately failed to mount a serious challenge.

Evolution of the Modern Engine

So before we launch into the innards of a modern Indy Car engine, it is interesting to chart the tracks of

Miller vs. Duesenberg

The contributions of Harry Miller and Fred Duesenberg to racing were not simply technological, but rather institutional. Because of these two men—who were motivated by completely different goals—the look and feel of racing changed.

The names of both Miller and Duesenberg appear on entry sheets at the Indianapolis Motor Speedway as early as 1913, but it was the post-war period around 1919 when the pair made their mark on racing—and not just American racing, but racing worldwide. Until then, the Indy Car series was really a competition based on cramming the best engine into the best car and racing that package at the Speedway. If Peugeot made the best engine/car combination, and the driver was good, well, that was the way it was.

But Miller and Duesenberg revolutionized thinking, making racing a different sort of sport. Oddly—and interestingly—they went about it from very different directions.

Miller had a technical background and was totally familiar with automotive design. Originally a carburetor manufacturer and supplier, his theories and his innovations came from firsthand knowledge of racing engines and racing cars. First entering racing as a carburetor supplier, then a fabricator of pistons and valves, Miller eventually came to create complete engines, then entire cars. Although adept in his own right, his ideas would be transformed onto paper by a team of master draftsmen—led by none other than Leo Goossen and Fred Offenhauser, creator of the famous "Offy" engine that would later dominate Indy.

It seemed that neither Goossen nor Offenhauser had any great love for racing, yet they were fantastic technicians and designers. Thus, when an imaginative idea came out of the mind of the racer, Miller, in was fed into the clinical shop of Offenhauser and Goossen. A look at the Miller shop in 1920 was like looking at a cafeteria, its benches spotless and its tooling in military style orderliness.

Duesenberg, on the other hand, was not involved in the process of building from start to finish. Duesenberg was also not as instinctive as Miller when it came to design. Duesenberg relied on an abstract vision of what the perfect race vehicle should be. Not blessed with the manpower or facilities that Miller had, Duesenberg made racing more a philosophy than a process. With his brother, August, Fred Duesenberg led a challenge to reduce the weight of the race car; he became obsessed with lightening the car from engine to chassis. To that end, Duesenberg used aluminum chassis frames with hardwood inserts to save weight. This design was far too crude for Miller, who used all-steel frames.

Duesenberg built race cars for a purpose other than winning races; he built cars to gain publicity, and he capitalized on his success with Duesenberg road car sales. The main goal, first and always, was to sell Duesenberg road cars. Miller, on the other hand, produced the best race cars money could buy, at one time even using Duesenberg chassis to win the Indy 500 with a Miller engine.

The differences in philosophy between Duesenberg and Miller produced differences in their final products. Miller's cars were always more sophisticated, with more "moving parts." His components were always made of the finest alloys available, with each piece of the component machined to very precise tolerances. (Miller was one of the first men to use chrome-moly for fabrication of race cars.) Miller would form simple pieces—such as connecting rods, wrist pins, etc.—from solid billets and machine them down to the right thickness, or he would cast seemingly insignificant parts to the exact shape he wanted. The cars were painstakingly assembled and created with as much attention as if they were sculpture.

But it was the Duesenberg straight eight engine that Miller copied and eventually perfected to beat Duesenberg. Developed for their passenger touring cars, the Duesenberg engine debuted in 1919 and was a throwback to more reliable and simpler engines of years earlier. Forsaking the dual overhead cam (DOHC) designs of the 1910s, it was a single overhead cam (SOHC) racing engine (although originally a pushrod engine). The engine was cast as a single unit incorporating crankcase, cylinders, and combustion chambers. The Duesenberg's guts were easily accessible and the compression was low, thereby keeping gasket failure to a minimum. The engine was successful... at the hands of Harry Miller.

Miller, who had experimented with four- and sixteen-cylinder engines, took the Duesenberg engine design—a 182ci SOHC eight, with battery ignition—and modified the bore/stroke relationship, shortening the stroke and increasing the bore. The engine won in a Duesenberg chassis at the hands of Jimmy Murphy in 1922. Finally, in 1924, with a 121ci, DOHC, nearly square-bore engine, Duesenberg finally captured the Indy 500 after some ten attempts. The Duesenberg would win twice more before racing's Golden Age would slide into oblivion at the end of 1929, with Miller taking the other three 500s.

The thirties and the era of frugality at Indy changed the emphasis from a high-tech spectacle to a "run-what-you-brung" show. In that climate, Duesenberg and Miller's cars were essentially obsolete. The new formula nearly bankrupted Miller, but he eventually returned in the mid-thirties with Ford to mount a challenge. Duesenberg, on the other hand, died in a road car accident. Without his leadership, the Duesenberg racing effort as well as the passenger car division faded away.

Six men over the wall at Phoenix. Races are often won and lost by these men, and not the ones in the drivers seat. Unfortunately, this team was not in that position and lightning quick pit work will still not help. The Alfa struggled to find power all season in 1992... and was rarely successful, posting one fourth place finish all year. Manufacturers such as

Porsche, Alfa, Buick and others often discover that engineering an Indy Car—even just the powerplant—is a much more difficult prospect than it first appears. This Alfa-Romeo-March effort was a disaster, even with Pat Patrick in charge and Danny Sullivan at the wheel. Miller Brewing

where it has been from a manufacturer's point of view. In other words, the Indy Car engine could have gone in a completely different direction were it not for the regulations of the sport's governing bodies and teams —which have always had an eye on making Indy Car racing a competitive series and a good show.

"Engine manufacturers spend almost as much on market research of that type as they spend on the program," says Kranefuss. "And you'll have to do this continuously as if there is no benefit. The technical benefits from working together with Cosworth is that we

have engineers working on those programs, and what they learn is not so much about high-performance technology, but they also learn about attitudes, which are completely different in racing, as opposed to the mainstream. You have a problem on a racetrack on Friday and you have to come up with an answer for Sunday. It may not be the right answer, but at least it will get you through the weekend. Whereas in the main stream, if you have a problem, there will be meetings, reviews, and so forth and so on. So it's a different approach, a different sense of urgency.

"In general, you can say that the value you get [in

The Chevy A (left), B (right), and C (center, back). Note the overall differences in size from one engine to the next. The trend has been to downsize the packages with each genera-tion. The engine's silhouette and its effects on the car's overall airflow make big differences in performance.

Indy Cars] versus any other series, [like, for example] in Formula One, is better. I think up until Honda came into Formula One, when all the manufacturers involved at that time, Renault, Ferrari, and maybe one or two others, were spending about the same amount of money on engine development. And then when Honda came, it took a different approach. Instead of spending 10 or 20 percent, they probably outspent us by over 500 or maybe 1,000 percent. There was obviously a completely different sense of value of the overall package. The same thing you can say if they [Honda] are coming to the Indy Car racing, and then using the same approach, they'll certainly will be able to do a lot of damage on the racetrack but in the process will do damage to the series.

"In Indy Car racing, we think we have a good understanding of what the overall value is, and I think we are pretty close in that respect to where General Motors is with their program. If somebody comes in and spends so much more, it upsets a very delicate balance, not only in terms of that company achieving

the success, but also in terms of upsetting the balance of the series."

'Secrets' of the Modern Engine

Cooperation between the CART and USAC boards would seem to guarantee that development on Indy Car engines would be fairly public. But there is a great deal of secrecy, and if even the mechanics don't know what's inside, it clearly becomes difficult to get concrete data to the public. With a little resourcefulness, however, we can give it a good try. So from the bottom up, here's a look at a modern Indy Car engine:

As mandated by the CART and USAC boards, these are the specifications as we know them: Maximum displacement is 161.703ci (2650ccm). Or for stock-block-derived pushrod engines, 209.3ci (3430 ccm). Although the pushrod engine class still exists, Buick, the leader in pushrod engines in Indy Car racing, essentially withdrew from competition in 1991. For our purposes here, the focus will be on the over-

Although the engines have been labeled as Chevrolets (at least they were; starting in 1993 they will be considered Mercedes engines), they are actually developed and built by Ilmor engineering. Shown here beside a Chevrolet C engine on an Ilmor dyno are Mario Illien (left) and Paul Morgan. Combining the first syllables of their last names gives you the name "Ilmor."

head cam engines, specifically the Ilmor and the Ford-Cosworth.

The maximum number of cylinders allowed in Indy Car competition is eight, the number which every car in the Indy Car ranks now uses. All are four-stroke, with one movement of the piston up or down in all four areas: intake, compression, power, and exhaust.

Engine Block

Both Ford and Ilmor blocks are made of aluminum and are cast in a process known as "sand-casting." The sand-casting varies between the two manufacturers, but Cosworth's patented operation was developed to provide a reliable way of making a high-integrity casting that could also be cast with thin walled sections.

With traditional die-casting (where there is a solid, reusable mold), the process creates a by-product that Cosworth calls a "turbulent transfer," which spreads fine particles of oxide throughout the casting. The particles ultimately act as a center for the forma-

tion of microporosity, or microscopic pitting. The pores make it difficult to keep a uniform integrity throughout the casting, which could result in weak spots. Since the engine acts as a stressed member of the entire package of the car, and is also cast with relatively thin walls, a poorly cast engine can lead to disastrous results.

This problem was addressed with two solutions. First, rather than drip the molten alloy into the mold from above, thus creating the "turbulent transfer," the mold is filled from below via an electromagnetic pump, a device originally developed for applications in the nuclear power industry. The casting contracts as it cools, but during the cooling process the pump continues to add molten metal to keep it from shrinking.

The mold itself must be made so that it will facilitate the expulsion of the oxide particles. Sand molds do that most effectively. The mold is actually created for the specific individual block and is designed to have nearly zero distortion. The sand Cosworth uses contains a high percentage of zircon, and sand of this quality is found only in Australia. It is very expensive, and is nearly 100 percent recyclable.

The sand is heated and formed into the mold of the block itself as well as the core, the inner portion of the mold that ultimately forms the water jackets. Then the metal is added to the mold through the electromagnetic pump. It is cooled and placed in a shake-out bed, where the sand deteriorates and falls cleanly from the casting. The block is then heat-treated, and the final product emerges.

There are really three ways to create parts out of metal: forging, billeting or machining, and casting. Billeting or machining guarantees the most consistent results. The billet, or hunk of raw metal, can be

The venerable Cosworth DFS, the last of the old breed. Michael Kranefuss, former director of Ford's worldwide racing division, said, "I think the reasons for the success of the V-8 in 1992 were basically the same as they were for the V-8 in 1967: The absence of anything else. There were not really any purpose-built engines around. We started winning with the Team Lotus, [and] we then made the engines available to almost anybody."

perfectly manufactured with the desired properties imbued. What Indy Car engine manufacturers contributed to the overall process of producing the engine came from the metallurgical side. They had discovered a process called metal matrixing, whereby cast metals molecularly form one of three patterns: face-centered cubic, box-centered cubic, or hexagonal close pack. In the first two cubic structures, the iron molecules bond themselves in boxes, and the hexagonal structure is a honeycombed-type chain of molecules. The box structures contain an inherent design flaw; as in any square concrete building, the metal may collapse under the wrong conditions or pressures.

Face-centered alloys tend to be more stable and will carry more weight, but the product does not cycle heat well. Box-centered alloys tend to be very stable in heat application. Hexagonal alloys tend to be more resilient and stronger, but also flex more than the other two. Titanium, for example, is a natural hexagonal close-pack metal.

So by taking an alloy that is one type of molecular structure and mixing it with other compounds—such as porcelain or beryllium, a heat resilient, lightweight

Chevy's "old" A V-8 exposed... to a certain degree. There are many secrets that will not be revealed here, secrets that haven't yet been revealed. However, as for oval pistons and metal matrixing, they are not allowed in Indy car racing.

The Famous 'Offy'

One of the most amazing histories in Indy Car racing concerns the little engine that refused to die—the Offenhauser, or Offy for short. The story of the Offy could (and does) fill the pages of an entire book all by itself. Its evolution and unbelievable fifty-year run is incredible in any context.

The engine won nearly 350 championship races, and countless sprint car races. At one point, from the middle of 1947 to the middle of 1964, the Offy had won all but three races (including one won by Louis Unser in a Maserati and one by Jimmy Clark in his Lotus Ford)—219 in all and 99 straight. But the fact that this powerplant survived for so long in the highly competitive racing arena says a great deal about its hardiness and its sound basic design.

The engine, an alternative to the Frontenac Fords that were so dominant on the dirt tracks of the early thirties, was essentially a converted Miller four-cylinder marine racing engine. A West Coast driver first lit on the idea, sensing that the Miller marine engine could be transformed into a lightweight, low-cost alternative to the Fronty-Ford.

The Miller engine, made for either 151ci or 183ci hydroplane racing, only cost about $1,000. Fred Offenhauser and Leo Goossen, working for Miller at the time, became interested in the idea and developed the engine for the sprint car. The engine was a winner in the car, and with the right transmission was capable of some very high speeds.

In 1930, Bill "Shorty" Cantlon qualified the car on the outside of the front row at Indy and finished second, then went on to finish second in the championship that season to Billy Arnold. In a few short weeks, Millers were being snapped up and Miller's shop was deluged with orders for replacement and aftermarket parts. Miller had struck upon a cheap racing engine for the privateer.

The engine was developed with the dual goals of both sturdiness and adaptability in mind. It was still a marine engine, but now could be used not only at Indy but on the banks of dirt tracks across the nation. It was powerful, producing perhaps 200hp with 10:1 compression ratios to run on pump fuel and benzol. It was cheap—$2,000 for a race-ready unit. It fit the Depression era perfectly.

The marine engine had some important assets from the beginning: it was powerful, delivering what Miller asked in power, but it was also compact and relatively lightweight, meaning it was efficient in an Indy Car and, mounted in a sprint car, nice and unobtrusive. The design was eventually changed slightly, incorporating bigger, tougher parts with some very important design changes that gave it its long life. The block and head combination was designed as a single unit, and the crankcase and crank bolted onto the bottom. It was fitted with four valves per cylinder and the bore/stroke was nearly squared, at 4.64x4.25. Everything—except the four-valve engine, which was designed during Miller's reign, but not produced until his departure—was provided for the grassroots racer.

By 1933, and in the wake of the new Indy regulations geared toward more frugal racing, Miller's business suffered. He had almost no interest in continuing the low-budget operations with the little four-cylinder engine. He filed for bankruptcy in 1933 and Fred Offenhauser purchased the tooling from Miller, forming the Offenhauser Engineering Company; Leo Goossen the genius at Miller, was rehired.

In the late thirties, Offenhauser Engineering increased the size of the engine to 270ci with a 4.36x4.63 bore/stroke combination. The compression ratio was raised to about 13:1, giving the engine nearly 300hp.

The threat from the new formula which allowed supercharging forced Offenhauser to look at re-inventing the Offy. Instead, he sold the company to three-time Indy winner Louie Meyer and Dale Drake in 1946, and they promptly hired Goossen again.

Even though the Offy was still competitive, they knew it wouldn't last. The supercharged cars were more powerful, but had enough design flaws to allow the Offy more wins than losses. The engine was generally strengthened, then fuel injected. By 1950 Meyer and Drake had introduced their supercharged engine—a 177ci, 8:1 compression engine. The engine now developed a prodigious 480hp at 6500rpm. In other words, it was close to the same horsepower figure of the larger, normally aspirated engine.

The engine, blessed with the same inherent compactness as when it was created in the twenties, lasted through the roadster age due to its ability to be laid on its side, thereby lowering both the center of gravity as well as the silhouette of the cowling.

When the engines were moved to the rear of Indy Cars in the mid-sixties, Ford created a V-8 to challenge the establishment. Drake and Goossen (Meyer had departed for Ford) faced the challenge squarely. They revised the supercharged engine, then actually offered a turbocharged version of it, and it produced more than 600hp. Although it would take some time to make it reliable, the engine—either supercharged or turbocharged—was back on top. At the 1968 Indy 500, Bobby Unser won the first race with the turbo Offy and, given the jump they had on Ford, the Offenhauser stayed dominant for several more seasons.

Finally, the Cosworth, which made its way from Europe, knocked the little engine off its perch. In 1975, the de-stroked turbo Cosworth made its debut, and its first win came a year later with Al Unser at the wheel. The Cosworth, which would revolutionize racing engines in its own right, would eventually be the powerplant of choice. Twenty-one months later, the Offenhauser was obsolete, winning its last race—after nearly fifty years of successful boat and automobile racing—at Trenton, New Jersey, with Gordon Johncock at the wheel.

The latest (and final, as far as Chevrolet badging is concerned) incarnation, the Chevrolet C engine. Engine designers do everything possible to keep the design secret. thus, most team members haven't got a clue as to what goes on below the cam covers. in any other form of American motorsports, the tuner obviously tunes the engine. Not so on an Indy Car. The engine is one area that is literally off limits to the team. They cannot see it, work on it, or fix it. All of that is left up to the manufacturers. The secrets, which seem to be well kept except between competing engine designers, are sequestered behind a mass of valve covers and plenums.

element often used as a moderator in nuclear reactors—the metal's inherent molecular structure is changed. The change is the metal matrixing, which actually forms sets of bridges, or matrixes, among the individual molecules. It fills in the spaces, and provides a bridge, or a frame, upon which the basic alloy can be strengthened.

It must be noted that CART no longer allows metal matrixing as it is now defined. No carbon fiber, metal matrix, or ceramic materials are allowed as

components. Engines must be strictly simple aluminum alloys and ferrous alloys, iron based or steel. This is meant to keep a lid on costs of remaining competitive. However, while researching metal matrixing, some interesting details came to light.

While there are three ways to create parts out of metal, there are also three basic ways to change the structure of a metal. The first, and simplest, is obviously with the alloy itself. The other methods are tempering and heat-treatment. Determining the makeup of a metal as the alloy is created yields a product with the most uniform texture. For example, a certain percentage of the alloy used in the manufacture of a normal racing block may contain a high percentage of silicon. This ensures that the metal of the block will have specific characteristics the engine designers seek and can rely upon when they calculate engine operating conditions.

A second way to change the characteristics of a metal lies in the way the metal is tempered, and a third is by a process known as heat-treatment. Alloys can take on the same essential forms as listed above if they are tempered—cooled—properly. If castings are the best way to form a complicated piece of metal, the heat it takes to melt it in preparation for casting will obviously change the makeup of the metal as it is being melted. A billet will have one property while cold, a second while molten, and a third as it finally cools after being cast. This is usually an undesirable situation.

But metallurgical engineers found that by quenching, or cooling, the metal in different ways, the metal forms different end products with different hypereutectic states. Hypereutectic is the creation of a certain "grain" of metal, essentially frozen in a particular state by the way the metal is cooled, or quenched. For example, a horseshoe magnet made of cast-iron has different qualities than a piece of iron staircase railing. A magnet is slivered and has a definite grain to it, while the railing has a different look and makeup. Yet staircase railings and magnets are formed of the same exact metals. How can that be? Through the different ways the metals are cooled for their respective applications.

In general, slowly cooled castings tend to be weak. The quicker they cool, the stronger they are, but they also tend to handle heat poorly. Go to a

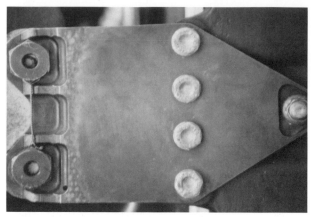

Although the engine is subjected to stress from the torque of the chassis under load as it races along, the chassis flexes only a little. However, with a powerplant with tolerances as tight as a Swiss watch, the flex proves significant.

foundry and ask what kind of steel they produce. They can hand you a catalogue with fifty pages of descriptions of the many types of steel available! (And there are many different ways of changing the metal, from liquid nitrogen quenching to cooling that takes several days.)

So, according to the rules, Indy Car blocks must be cast of "monolithic" alloys—in other words, no porcelain or exotic chains of metals. The old way to create a block was to die-cast it, creating a porosity that for the most part was evident even to the naked eye. If you have ever looked at the inside of a block from the bottom end, you can imagine how it would feel to the touch: rough and gritty, like sandpaper. With nearly any casting process there is bound to be a rough surface, but the differences between a sand casting and a die-casting are like night and day. The sand casting creates a surface that is *much* smoother. As long as they contain the inherent strength of a cast part, the smoother the surfaces, the better the part.

Fluid and air pass around smooth surfaces much better than they do around rough surfaces. Of course, the porosity affecting the structural integrity is also enhanced with the sand casting process. And modification can be done on the block design with a lead time of only about six weeks.

Even though the engines run fairly cool, they are simultaneously cooled further by water (with only a stop leak added, no coolant) from the bottom of the engine on the Cosworth. Water is pumped into the engine at the lower front end of the engine, from both sides. It travels upward through the engine through the top front end of the cylinder heads, through a set of swirl heads to remove the air from the water, and then through the pod-mounted radiators to begin the cycle all over again at the bottom of the block.

Again, the block is a stressed member of the

The engine is attached to the chassis by just a few bolts. The engine is actually a stressed member of the chassis, bearing the loads of the entire platform of the race car. The chassis is essentially the cockpit and all the mounting points of the suspension. Nevertheless, it is the chassis design that can truly make or break a season.

The Novi Story: Power and Potential

As rich in history—yet perhaps not as successful—as the Offenhauser engine, was the Novi engine that was to blaze around the ovals of America, wowing crowds of race fans in the process.

The Novi is remembered as an engine of the sixties, and is mostly associated with the name Granatelli. Yet the Novi was actually born in pre-war America, in 1940. Ed and Bud Winfield of Winfield Racing Carburetors wanted a strong engine capable of handling a supercharger. Lou Welch, who sold rebuilt Ford engines, helped in the project—as did legendary Leo Goossen. Welch, who had a hand in the financing, got his wish to name the engine after his hometown—Novi, Michigan.

Goossen designed the original Novi engine and it was an awful lot like the Offy—with barrel crankcase and integral block and head casting. The 90 degree design didn't do well in the Miller chassis that was set up for the 1935 Indy 500. The extra weight of the big Novi hurt the Miller's handling and the engine never worked to its potential.

When World War II ended, Goossen got back to work on a front-drive transmission specifically for the Novi and, mated with a new chassis, the new Novi car set the track record at Indy shortly after its introduction. Again, however, the logistics of running a huge, powerful V-8 conspired to keep the Novi from winning. The overpowered beast, which absolutely screamed down the straight-aways, wore tires horribly and it was constantly stopping for fuel. Even though it was faster than the competition, in the long run it was slower. And even though the team fitted the monster with a huge, 115-gallon fuel tank, the Novi was still in the pits more than any other car.

The problems of tire wear were never overcome and the front-driver was essentially a piece of potentially successful—yet undeveloped—machinery.

Welch contracted Frank Kurtis to build a rear-drive chassis to accommodate the Novi. The car might have won the 1956 Indy 500 were it not for a tire failure. By the following season the Kurtis chassis was out of date and the Novi was out of the running again.

Welch gave up. He had had enough. But Andy Granatelli decided the car still had potential—with a bit of tweaking—and he bought the Welch operation, lock, stock, and barrel.

Granatelli cleaned up the supercharger design, thereby enhancing performance, gaining power to the tune of about 650hp. But the Kurtis chassis was still a problem. It could hardly hold the less powerful engine of four seasons earlier, so it would certainly not work with the rejuvenated Novi.

The answer was four-wheel-drive. Inspired by a conversation with Stirling Moss, who had the opportunity to drive an all-wheel-drive Grand Prix car, Granatelli contacted Ferguson, a British four-wheel-drive manufacturer.

The 700-plus horsepower was transmitted through a centrally located differential and it looked strong. But the weight of the car still made tire wear an issue. In addition, Bobby Unser, who drove the car in 1964 and 1965, did not find the outright speed of the car better than the rear-drive Novi, all things considered.

The car qualified at Indy in 1964 and 1965, but dropped out once due to crash and once due to a mechanical problem. In 1966 Unser jumped ship, and the Novi was not able to qualify that year. It died having never won a championship Indy Car race. It is, however, still an integral part of Indy's history.

---

chassis. The cockpit monocoque—lies ahead of the engine and includes the driver safety compartment, all the tubing or carbon fiber components made to stiffen the cockpit, the front suspension, fuel tank, etc. Behind the driver, then, is the engine, which is essentially bolted directly onto the rear bulkhead of the race car. There is no frame. The transmission is bolted onto the end of the engine, and the rear suspension and rear wing are bolted onto the end of the transmission.

Although the engine is subjected to stress from the torque of the chassis under load as it races along, the chassis flexes only a little. However, with a power plant with tolerances as tight as a Swiss watch, even that minuscule amount of flex proves significant.

"We had to take that all into consideration," says Bisco, "because there's going to be twisting moments and flexing moments. They originally started off with the same blocks between the two engines, but then typically high-speed ovals would put fatigue cracks in the blocks in certain places, so we ended up making a design change in the block in certain places. You nev-

The cooling system features a pair of radiators. This one is exposed here, but they sit inside the side pod bodywork when the car is on the track. Cool liquid is pumped through the bottom of the engine and flows upward.

A crew member removed the plugs, which is one of the few engine chores the team can undertake itself. The bulk of the building, development, tuning, and rebuilding is left to the engine suppliers from whom the teams lease their powerplants.

er see that problem in Formula One [with the Cosworth], but you see it all the time in Indy Car racing. [The stress is usually] between the rear cylinders and the bell housing. The engineers would do an analysis on it. And you didn't want to fix the back [cylinders] and have it [the stress] move on along to the next ones, so we re-engineered it.

"Our engine has all of the drives from the crankshaft up to the camshaft, and the auxiliary pumps and things are all on the front of our engine. Ilmor has done it the other way around. When Ilmor first came out, they had all their valve gear on the front of the engine, and put it on the back of the engine. Rumor suggests that they were getting a lot of flex there and it was causing a lot of ignition and driveline problems."

Not all chassis flex can be eliminated. Since the Indy engine is considered a part of the chassis, buffering the shock is taken up through the wheels and through the crankshaft.

It is too time-consuming and expensive to repair a block that has suffered a massive failure. The engines are leased, rather than purchased, primarily because the manufacturers want to ensure quality. When a massive failure occurs, the manufacturers would rather just replace the block than risk another failure while trying to save some money.

Part of the block is meant to be replaceable, however. The wet liners that protect the block from scoring are completely obsolete after fewer than 1,000 miles due to their unique metal makeup. They are made of an aluminum alloy with a hard surface on the running side. Called wet liners because they come in direct contact with the liquid that cools the

engine, the liners are the source of some stuttering and back-peddling by designers. There are "special surfaces that are very hard" in the liners, is about all they'll divulge. Since coatings are allowed by CART rules, the surfaces could be anything from nikasil to porcelain.

Crank, Rods, Bearings, and Pistons

So the crank has several roles. It serves as the buffer for the flex in the chassis; it drives the cam, timing, and virtually all the other gears at the front of the motor; and it drives the car. Tough job.

Made of the English RR56 alloy, the crank is forged from one piece, heat-treated, and tuftrided. The tuftriding process imparts some hardness to the journal surface holding the increased bearing loads. Tuftriding is a dry lubricant which allows metals to slide against each other without additional lubrication. It also stabilizes the crank.

The 25in crank is supported by five main bearings. So although it flexes a bit, the movement is not significant. According to Mike Wolther, an engine rebuilder at Hall-VDS, the cranks, at least on the Chevys and the old DFXs, have few problems. "They just don't break," he says.

The crank has a gear that drives a "tower" of gears which eventually end up at the camshaft. On the Cosworth, it's on the front; on the Chevy, it's at the back.

Holding the pistons in place are steel connecting rods. They are usually forged. Titanium rods were used at one time, but CART has since banned their

Spark plugs used in Indy Cars are similar to any street car plugs. "Reading" the plugs is not really a viable way to determine what is happening in the engine anymore—at least not with current technology. Instead, there's a wealth of data provided by the cars' electrical systems, which monitor practically every aspect of performance.

use because of costs Now they are steel. Aluminum is not used because it does not have the integrity to last for 500 miles. On the front straights of Indy or Road America, with the revs reaching and often exceeding 13,000rpm, the rods tend to move and perhaps pound the crank. Under those circumstances, eventually the engine will lose a bearing. The rods do tend to twist occasionally—most likely from heat cycling—when they heat up and bend. A standard test by engine builders is what's called a "bend and twist" test. They have to be within certain specifications or they can't be used; typically, eight- to ten-thousandths (.008-.010in) is the limit of tolerance.

Bore and stroke on an average Ilmor Chevy C engine is 88x54.4mm, with a compression of about 11:1. The short stroke does two things: It enables the car to have a very high powerband with a great rev capability of somewhere around 12,900rpm, and it also allows the crank to have a short profile, which lowers it and gives it a lower center of gravity. Why is an Indy Car piston usually 11:1 when turbo engines usually require a drop in compression? Since the Indy Car runs only about 7lb per square inch more than sea level pressure, the engines can be tuned almost as though they are normally aspirated engines.

The dry sump lubrication system allows the engine to operate without an oil pan. Instead, the oil is stored in an outside container, pumped through the system, collected again, and deposited in the oil tank for redistribution.

Pistons are round forged aluminum alloy, with three rings—two scrapers and one oil (oval pistons are not allowed by CART and USAC). Before forging, Cosworth pistons are given an initiation of sorts: the billet is hit with a 500-ton weight to give it additional resilience.

The skirting is a secret, with different configurations used for different applications. A piston that a team would run in a 500-mile race would not likely be the same one that would be run in a 300-mile road race. For a longer race, the pistons might be made of a heavier-duty alloy or of a different design to last, which would inhibit the revs a bit. Much of that difference has to do with skirting. Another secret with pistons concern the coatings—which are still legal and are closely guarded secrets. Over the course of a year, the engine might have several different pistons. But usually by the beginning of the next season, there are only a couple of choices. The effective designs have been incorporated and the poor performing parts will be abandoned.

Head, Cam, and Valves

Like the block, Indy Car cylinder heads are sand-cast aluminum alloy. And although the exact design of the head is confidential, it is certainly a pent-roof design. The four valves per cylinder come in at an angle of a little less than 45deg.

Cosworth has also been able to avoid almost all

the inevitable mutations of the metal as it is moved and machined after the casting is completed. Traditional methods for a complex casting meant clamping and machining, then reclamping and remachining a half-dozen times. Unless it is reclamped in the exact manner each time, the metal will distort. Cosworth developed a method whereby the casting is held in a frame, allowing all four sides to be reached by the tools, so the casting is never unclamped until the finished product is snapped out.

Liquid nitrogen is frequently used to shrink the valve seats before they are inserted into the heads. Once the seats are in place, they will be heated again to room temperature to ensure a precise fit. The cutting of the seats is an insidious process that makes a single machining impossible. The "plunge" into the metal makes the geometry not quite right, and performance suffers down the road. Instead of a direct-action machine, Cosworth uses a single-point diamond bit with a curved tool, which creates a perfectly shaped seat. At the same time, the tool aligns a tappet bore tool, which coincides perfectly with the valve seat. The roundness of the seat is usually held to within 10 microns.

Indy Cars do not have head gaskets. Both engines seal the combustion chamber with a set of rings—like O-rings—that fit around each cylinder atop the block. What looks like a wire ring is actually a square section only a few thousandths of an inch thick that sits on the block. When the head is torqued down against

Water is added prior to practice. "Not only do we not [fix the engine], we're not allowed to do that," explained one crewman. "Under the lease program, nobody really owns their own engines. Chevy and Ford say, 'You don't take anything apart unless we have a person there'. I have had occasion to take valve covers off because we've broken a drive to the fuel pump of something like that, but you don't do any of that unless there's a designated person there."

Ready to be rebuilt, this engine was just separated from the car. Unlike some forms of racing, where considerable engine work is done on-site, In Indy Car racing, engines are never rebuilt at the track. They are simply separated from the car, put under plastic tarps and shipped back to the supplier to be torn down, rebuilt, and re-sealed. The average teardown is done at about 500-mile intervals and it will cost about $40,000 per rebuild.

the block, it forms a seal that will not be broken unless the block overheats—in which case, it will melt into the block. Very rarely will the rings melt through; they will simply dissolve or melt.

Like anything else in the engine, the rings are susceptible to heat. Life expectancy depends on how many times the engine is exposed to heat and how many cycles it goes through. Once a ring gets soft—once it just begins to melt—it is on its way out. It is a deteriorating substance. "It definitely has a life," says Wolther. "A lot of it is down to how well the team takes care of their stuff."

Valves are usually made of titanium. The 500-mile races are run with something else, though, most likely just a steel valve with a coating similar to that of the wet liners. Steel is used for ultimate dependability rather than short-term performance.

One of the most amazing things about this engine—at least one which can be conceived without seeing the inside of an engine—is the operation of the steel valve springs. The springs are "steel, but that's all I can tell you," says Wolther. But thinking about the conditions under which these springs have to operate boggles the mind.

Bear in mind that in Grand Prix racing, compressed-air valvetrains have been found to be the only way to operate the valves as the engine's ability to rev continues to improve. Formula One designers decided that at 12,000rpm, the revs were far too high for a spring to handle without having a problem with the valve "floating." The spring is compressed and released so quickly that it never really has time to rebound. If the design of the spring is flawed, the consequences to the engine can be literally catastrophic. So while Formula One cars use compressed air to

open and close the valves, that technology was outlawed in Indy Cars due to cost. What Indy Car engine designers accomplish is done with apparently common metals. It is the design process that is secret.

"It's actually not that difficult to do," explains Paul Ray of Ilmor. "It's a straightforward set of sums. The lighter you can make it, the easier it moves. Inertia kills you. It's not the speed, but the inertia, that you're fighting. It comes down to camshaft hardness and the acceleration of the valves, not the velocity of the valves. That can be accomplished through a lightening process.

"As long as you can reduce the weight, you could go on to infinity. I'm sure twenty years ago if someone said you could run a four-stroke at 14,000rpm, you'd have said it was ridiculous. But now we're looking at maybe in the future getting up there even farther."

Ray still sticks to the official Ilmor line of 12,900rpm as the rev limit, but some drivers report that they have overrevved the engine quite substantially—up to 16,000rpm—without failure.

This is astounding performance, considering that Grand Prix motorcycles use reed valves on their two-stroke engines because designers couldn't figure out a better way to get the fuel in and the exhaust out. In motorcycle engineering, technology is normally light-years ahead, but the reed valve is nothing more than a carbon fiber or aluminum flap that lets air in as the engine is on the intake/compression stroke. Bike engines rev only a little higher than Indy Car engines.

As Ray explained, the capacity for revving has a great deal to do with the camshaft. The cam has to be extremely hard to keep the springs opening at the high revs for a sustained period, but the cam itself is nothing special. In other words, it doesn't look like something that would be very powerful. It looks only slightly dissimilar to a street car cam.

Like the crank, camshafts are made of tuftrided steel. They are pretty hardy components, rarely suffering failure. The cam followers never leave the lobe, which is critical due to the revs of the engine. Variable timing is forbidden in Indy Cars, so any change in the system is done through the electronic ignition, not through the camshaft.

A trigger off the cam sends data to the black box that changes the way the engine will run by controlling the amount of fuel the engine gets or the degree to which the ignition is advanced or retarded. Run off the electrical system, the box controls and records the rpm for the driver as the car comes back in the pits after practice or up on a video screen via live-time telemetry.

Also run off the electrical system are the fuel injectors. These are checked after each race, are put into a dummy plenum, and are always flowed as a set. The injectors operate separately and are controlled individually by a set of wires running directly to the individual injectors. Each injector has an impulse to tell it to inject. Like the electronic ignition on a street car that exists just for reference, a mock schematic gives the injection system something to verify its order with. The injectors do not simply pour fuel into the runners all the time. This is a timed injection system that knows where the piston is in the stroke and delivers the fuel accordingly. Fuel is not sprayed directly on the back of the valves. How far do the runners move the fuel? Another secret. "Farther than you'd think," says Wolther with a laugh.

Fuel is injected before top dead center, but the design of the plenum (which will be addressed more in the chapter on turbos)—as well as that of the gear train and other internal workings—is a closely guarded secret.

Part of the Package

The old DFX engine which ran successfully from the mid-seventies to the late eighties was a derivative of another engine, actually manufactured for another formula. It was originally a Formula One engine, a 3ltr DFZ destroked in the early days of the Indy Car market. It ran 80-100in of boost, and produced about 1000hp. But its rpm was very low (8000rpm) relative to what Ford is running now. Over the years, the cars have become quicker and the sanctioning bodies have gradually brought the boost down. As the boost came down, the rpm compensated for it.

Now they're running at up to 13,000rpm with 45in of boost. The original engine wasn't designed to rev that high, so the engine was redesigned.

At the same time, the car's aerodynamics were drastically improved. The front of the engine was reduced so that the car could be kept smaller. And the Ford engine was probably the biggest one available, compared to Judd, Alfa-Romeo, Porsche, and Buick. The Ilmor that came out originally was about 4in lower and about 5in narrower than the original Ford engine—prompting Ford and Cosworth to get back to work. The result was the XB, which, aerodynamicists insisted was the "slipperiest" engine to slice through the Brickyard air.

"To give you an idea of what a difference the compactness makes to the car," Bisco explains, "one of our designers said that [at] 230mph, the difference between the old car and the new car—by making it smaller behind the driver so you don't have as much area to cut through the wind—is like giving the engine another 20hp."

That's a great deal of power to gain. The trend was to lighten and continue to downsize, but the rules are thwarting that downsizing trend in the interest of fuel efficiency and cost savings.

"Typically with the older engine, there was a mechanical loss at high rpm," says Bisco. "It was really high. So a lot of attention was put on designing a low friction characteristic in the engine. This helps, especially at the high rpm range."

Indy 500 winner Arie Luyendyk has driven a variety of race cars, including the original Cosworth, the Chevy A, the Nissan GTP car, the Jaguar XJR10, and the new Cosworth XB. What was the difference between the packages, and how *does* it feel to drive some of these engines?

"The 1991 Chevy engine I drove was a different Chevy. The A [had a much better top end than] the old Ford Cosworth. I noticed that at places like Michigan and Indianapolis. The Ford engine seems to pick up at very low rpms. It is very driveable at low revs—I'm talking about 5000[rpm]. It's a bit more driveable and has a bit more response than the Chevy. It also mattered what car you had it in. We had it in the Lola. The '91 Lola compares differently to the '92.

"The Jaguar had a lot of torque, but it only started at 6500[rpm]. Anything below [that], and there was nothing there. You always had to keep high revs—like at about 7000[rpm]. But then once it got going, it was a lot of torque. And there wasn't that

Arie Luyendyk has had experience with several different types of powerplants. He drove the original Cosworth, the Chevy A, a Nissan GTP car, the Jaguar XJR10 and the new Cosworth XB. "The power band is actually very, very short on all of these engines," Luyendyk says. "They make their power in the area of about 12,000[rpm] up to 12,500[rpm], somewhere in that area, so that's where you find most of the drivers feel is in the top end of these things. I mean, you've got power and driveability there."

much top speed compared to the turbo cars.

"The power band is actually very, very short on all of these engines. They make their power in the area of 12,000 to 25,000 [rpm], somewhere in that area, so that's where most of the drivers [think they will find] the top end, and I'm like anybody else. But in Indy Cars, the power band is wide—from 5000[rpm] to 28,000[rpm]. Power. I mean, you've got power and driveability there."

A Champion's Impressions

Al Unser, Jr. has also driven several race cars, winning the 24 Hours of Daytona in a Porsche 962C, racing a Chevy GTP and Chevy C, and testing a Williams Formula One car.

"I've driven all different types of race cars," Unser says. "The differences between Williams and the Indy Car is [that with] the Williams, all the power was on the bottom end of the engine. Even though it turned a lot more rpm, it still accelerated very, very quickly, and so there was no comparison, really. The IMSA Porsche 962 is just another IMSA car. The IMSA car and the Indy Car are pretty close, as far as putting the power to the ground. The down force is so much greater in the IMSA car than [in] the Indy Car. And I think mechanically, the Indy Car puts it down better. The Porsche had a lot of turbo lag in it, because they ran intercoolers for the turbo. It had to go through the turbo and then through an intercooler, and then to the engine, whereas the Indy Car goes directly to the plenum and the turbo's not that very far away."

The evolution of the Indy Car is a conglomeration

Some things have never been allowed into Indy Car racing. For instance, the pneumatic valvetrain that was developed for Formula One racing has less moveable and breakable parts, but the cost added to the engine can be prohibitive, and only the wealthiest teams would be able to develop the technology. IndyCar made the decision not to allow that technology. Note the safety wiring around the top rim of the pop-off valve and how the hoses carrying the car's fuel run through the bulkhead to the engine (left).

of sorts between past Indy Car engines and the trick gadgetry on newer GTP turbos. The hybrid power plant still moves forward quickly—both figuratively and literally.

"The technology is way ahead of what it used to be," Luyendyk says. "On the old Cosworth, as opposed to the new Cosworth, at 12,500[rpm], you were really stretching it. I mean, 11,800[rpm] was really about what you wanted it at. And now you're 1,100 revs higher. And it happened so smoothly, you know. Voom, it just goes right up there. There's no hiccup, there's no resistance."

Cosworth engineers figure that if the car is sitting in the pits revving at, say, 3000rpm and the throttle is stabbed, the engine will go to perhaps 5000rpm in one turn of the crankshaft. At the same time, the reliability of the new engines has gotten better over the years.

"On the straight-away at Indy, for instance, you get to a point where you hit this wall, this imaginary wall, where the engine just kind of stops.," Luyendyk comments. "It's peaked out and it just doesn't accelerate anymore. The Ford Cosworth took it a step further where it accelerated down almost into turn one. The Chevy [A engine] peaked out at start/finish [line] almost. The Ford just kept accelerating and accelerating. Also, the acceleration off the corner was better. So at a high rpm, we could still accelerate off the corner better."

Unser carries this assessment one step farther. "The great advance in reliability has really come from the electronics, from the engine. You do not have to adapt to anything. You can just drive the car that much harder, all day long. So it gives you a lot of confidence to go out and just run it, and run it hard all day."

Racers want the engine to supply smooth power with good reliability. But if they could get a big, overweight engine that could power the most efficiently bodied car to a record speed at the Indianapolis Motor Speedway, they'd trade the new technology in the blink of an eye.

"Every year they get more power out of them," explained Luyendyk. "So every year they think there's something they can do by either lightening stuff by [using] different materials [or] by making the engine out of different materials. Of course, you'll have more rpm [and that] usually relates to speed. The rpms are up over [those of] a couple of years ago. A couple of years ago, you were running 11,500, [and] now you're running 12,900.

"The engines have come a long way, but it's not just the engines. The aerodynamics make a car go quick, too. We were going fast back then anyway, but we had too much down force then and we needed more power to pull us through. A lot has to do with aerodynamics. The cars are a lot sleeker, so they go through the air quicker, which doesn't require as much horsepower. If you're going to ask me how it

CHEVY INDY V8/A   **CHEVY INDY V8/C**

This head-on look at two Chevrolet (Ilmor) engines shows how designers have streamlined the silhouettes of engines as they've helped them evolve. The Chevy A on the left was considered fairly efficient, yet consider how much less space the C on the right would take up in an Indy Car. The more compact the engine, the more aerodynamic the car's bodywork, and the less drag it generates. It's remarkable, really, to see how engine designers have been able to reduce the mass of the powerplants considering that they're working with some pre-determined factors such as displacement limits. Everything's got to work more efficiently when the size of components such as cylinder heads and manifolds is reduced. Chevrolet

was in 1989, I can tell you that if we had the power that we have today back then, we would have been going a lot quicker at Indy.

"But we haven't really had to adjust ourselves. Like when I went from a Cosworth—the old Cosworth—to a Chevy, you didn't have to adjust your driving, you just wanted more power." Then he added with a grin, "Everybody wants more power."

Pop-off valves are allotted each morning and collected each afternoon after the final session or race. Drivers and teams have often complained about valves which are not set quite right—obviously only if they are set to open with less pressure than allotted.

Notice the popoff valve sticking out of Danny Sullivan's Galles. "You want to make sure you don't blow the pop-off, because it's a big hole," says Randy Bain of Galles Racing. "There are springs that control that. When they say 'turning up the boost,' there are knobs in the cockpit that have lines that connect back to the wastegate so the driver can either add or take air off the top of the wastegate 'can' and make it more efficient. You end up blowing the wastegate instead of the popoff valve."

There were really only two engines in the 1993 season that had a chance to take the championship, and on any given race weekend the odds-on favorites were teams who had use of one of those two powerplants—either the Ilmor engine, originally called the Chevrolet A, B, or C engine, and the Ford Cosworth XB engine. To lease either an Ilmor or Cosworth engine in 1993 would have cost around $150,000 for the year. Shown here are silhouettes of the "old" Cosworth DFS engine (outside engine; solid line) and the newer generation Ford-Cosworth XB engine (inside engine; dotted lines). Cars using the newer engine benefitted from the smaller, lower package.

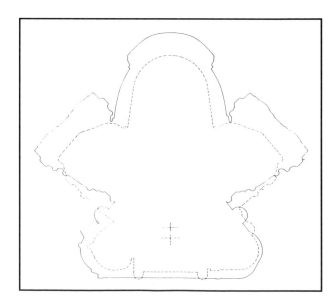

The ultimate "spacer" as it sits waiting to be replaced. "For us, the engine is just a big spacer in the middle of the car," says Randy Bain, a mechanic who worked for several years with Galles Racing. "If it works, fine. If it doesn't, well, we'll just get another spacer."

Chapter 5

Power Squared: The Turbochargers

In 1908, a somewhat historically forgettable fellow named Lee Chadwick built a belt-driven gizmo which purported to suck air in and more or less ram it into the intake manifold. By the best reports, Mr. Chadwick produced almost no gains in power—even though the idea was fundamentally sound. He was the first racer to use supercharging in any practical application on a race car—this, a few seasons before the first race at Indy.

The first experiments with the device at Indy were done by Mercedes, which used roots-type superchargers that pushed air into the intake manifold. Later, Duesenberg fitted its cars with a centrifugal blower, and Joe Boyer won driving a Duesie in 1924. Early analysis of the first superchargers, or blowers as we now call them, indicated that they produced 3-4lb per square inch, and were probably 10 percent efficient, meaning that of the air being impelled into the manifold, only 10 percent or so actually reached the cylinder. There was perhaps a 5 percent potential gain in horsepower with this noisy vacuum-clear-type apparatus, but the blower usurped nearly the same amount of energy trying to drive the blower. The gains were almost nil. Yet they sounded so great, everybody had to have one.

The trouble was that at supersonic rotor speed, internal sonic booms were generated. Harry Miller developed an approach to eliminate the cause of the trouble by redesigning the inducer vanes of the impeller. Boost pressures rocketed to 20psi.

So the story of supercharging went. And until 1952, it was the means to enhance performance. But Cummins Engine Company took advantage of the AAA regulations and developed a diesel engine for competition at the Brickyard. It failed the first year due to a supercharger problem and had to be withdrawn. In an attempt to overcome those problems, the supercharger was dumped the following season in favor of a turbocharger. The Cummins Diesel broke the track's lap record and took the pole for the start of the 1952 race.

The turbo was a revolutionary device that used the exhaust gases to turn the impeller rather than using the engine speed to drive a supercharger. Although the Cummins turbo ended up sucking dirt and debris off the track, clogging itself until the unit seized and died, the turbocharger had caught the attention of every engineer in the paddock. The initial turbo was a huge thing that developed only about 15psi, but gave the diesel some 400hp.

The early turbos were primitive fans, driven off the exhaust. As the exhaust gas built up pressure, the impeller fan spun faster, forcing air into the manifold with more velocity. It was as simple as that. There was no variation and no cooling. Talk about turbo lag: it took about 5sec for the turbo to build up speed; the throttle had to be applied in anticipation of the car moving out of the turn—5sec in advance.

We now know something of what an unrestricted turbo can do. The Honda Grand Prix turbo, which won the World Championship in 1988, was rumored to develop almost 2000hp during qualifying—with a 1.5ltr engine. Unlimited power for unlimited pocketbooks.

The same was true in Indy Car racing. Every time USAC—or by the early-eighties, CART—limited the boost or intake on a turbo, engineers found a way to make the turbo more efficient. In fact, the biggest impetus to make advancements came from the rules makers trying to make the turbos obsolete. They failed. The designers just found a way to make the less-efficient units efficient. Finally, the intake was reduced so much and the pop-off valves (more about pop-off valves in a minute) are made so accurate that the gains in turbocharging have been steadily abated. Improvements in overall performance have come recently from the engine itself, not the way it breathes.

Inside Turbos

To get an idea of how turbos work, you'll need to understand what "inches" are and what it means to reduce them. "Inches" refers to inches of mercury. Ambient atmospheric pressure at sea level will support a column of mercury in a tube to the height of 29.9in. In pounds-per-square-inch, that means 14.7lb, which is one atmosphere at sea level. When a driver says he is limited to 45in of boost (the 1993 regulation), he is speaking of the total allowance. More simply put, at 45in, the driver is limited to one-and-a-half times the pressure outside the car. In the early-seventies, boost was up to about 110in, and horsepower was reaching 1,050 for short qualifying blasts. By 1974, the boost had been limited to 80in and was governed by the new pop-off valve. The boost has since been further restricted, but engine output remains in the 850hp area.

How does it work on a current Indy Car? Intake for the turbo is brought in through a duct in the bodywork, and the air comes into that duct. The first thing it encounters is the cold side wheel, which is spinning because the exhaust is pushing the wheel on the other side of the shaft. It draws it in, and then sucks it down into the engine. Depending on the car—some bring air in on the side, some bring it in through the top—the new air has to travel only a few inches before it gets to the fan blades.

The intake side is the simple-to-explain side of the intake/exhaust equation. The other side, the driven exhaust fan, is the more complicated part of the apparatus.

Exhaust is expelled through the exhaust valves out of the heads, and the burnt fuel mixed with air begins its journey out the pipes and into the atmosphere. It is expelled with some force. The force through the tubes is free energy. The turbo, then, harnesses some of that fast-moving air by means of a fan blade mounted inside what is essentially a part of the exhaust pipe.

The turbo is a fairly straightforward device that tends to have many critical failure areas. In fact, the entire unit is prone to failure at almost any time. It has to be made as tough as possible to withstand the heat and friction wear that spinning at 100,000rpm will cause. Typical turbo problems are caused by a misread of the proper relationship between feed pressure and scavenge capability. In other words, a pump in the engine pumps oil up to the turbo. It *must* be set at the right volume and pressure. The size and flow capacity of the line is also important. The same is true on the scavenge side. A scavenge pump on the engine removes oil from the turbo. So, it both pushes it in and sucks it out.

The turbine wheels are made of aluminum, and the spin-on bearings are made of impregnated bronze. A pressure feed injects oil into the top, and a combination of gravity and pressure drops it down through several different galleys and glands, finally feeding the bearings, ultimately sucked out at the bottom. The whole pressure area is about the size of an orange.

There are no intercoolers on today's Indy Cars. The two sanctioning bodies simply didn't want the expense. Consequently, the units will sometimes glow red-hot. Considerable heat is being forced down into a small area, and with its spinning and compressing, the turbo builds up a great deal of heat.

As noted earlier, the old turbos simply used the gasses to spin the turbine. The new turbos, however, use a much more sophisticated set of controls to vary the force that travels along the pipe housing the turbo fan. That variable control consists mostly of the wastegate.

The wastegate is essentially a valve in the exhaust. As the exhaust comes off the engine, a small piece of secondary tubing is mounted alongside the primary pipes. That's where the wastegate is:—mounted in a 2-2.25in opening. On the top side of the pop-off valve is a spring—a diaphragm—that's interconnected to the intake plenum. When the plenum gets to 45in—or to a said given point—the wastegate lets pressure out the exhaust. Why not just allow the pop-off valve to deploy and allow the air out that way?

"The wastegate is variable because it has springs in it, [and] the springs just don't open like that," Arie Luyendyk says. "They gradually open and shut. They've put a lot of work into the wastegates and things like that. I mean, yeah, it comes on with a bang at one point, but you can gradually feed it in and drive it like an atmospheric car. It depends on what snail—turbo housing—you have on the car. Cosworth has done a few things with regard to how the power comes in and how the turbo comes in. They play around with all kinds of things to make it driveable."

"You want to make sure you don't blow the pop-off, because it's a big hole," says Randy Bain from Galles Racing. "There are springs that control that. When they say 'turning up the boost,' [they are referring to] knobs in the cockpit that have lines that connect back to the wastegate so the driver can either add or take air off the top of the wastegate 'can' and make it more efficient. You end up blowing the wastegate instead of the pop-off valve."

The wastegate valve fits in the secondary tubing in the exhaust; on top of it is a spring and what's called a "can." The lines from the cockpit go to the top of the can to regulate it and everything that is interconnected with the plenum. It's changed via a standard 3/16in Dash Four vacuum line.

Bain continues, "If [a driver] has too much boost, he'll wind the knob in, which reduces the air to the top of the can. If he wants to add boost, he'll add [it] to the top of the can. If he's waiting until the end of the race to turn the boost up, he needs to be fired because he should have adjusted it the first lap," Bain adds with a laugh. "You optimize boost right away. Unless something happens, that's hardly ever adjusted.

"Turning the boost up or down is kind of a thing of the past. That was something they did back when they ran the engines with enough inches where it made a difference. But now, with 45in, you just want to optimize it. You don't do anything to change your fuel mileage. That's all done with the adjustment on the dash where [the driver] can adjust the mix percentage of fuel and air."

Providing Big Gains in Power

The turbo has been a source of incredible gains in power in the past. In fact, for two decades, a great deal of the advances in racing came from the induction systems and the updated superchargers and turbochargers. Since intercoolers were banned from Indy Car competition, innovators have had to turn their focus to some other areas of the turbo. Some car builders tried ceramic wheels, which were quickly outlawed, again in the attempt to keep costs down. But one thing they have done to improve performance the most is to make the size of the compressor housing itself smaller. That reduces the lag time between when the gas is applied and the driver actually gets full boost.

The Truesports car used a different setup for turbo intake in 1992. Turbo inlets on most cars are incorporated into the body work as slits or ducts. Here, the intake hangs out of the bodywork. The designers must hope that the benefits of the turbo more than offset the aerodynamic price paid for a component that sticks out into the air like this.

Nevertheless, the power curve of turbo cars has improved by leaps and bounds. Where the old cars took as much as a few seconds to develop power, the newer turbos come on gradually but with almost instantaneous power, building into a nice, usable torque range.

"What happened," Emerson Fittipaldi says, "is that the present turbo engine has the same torque and power of the old, normally aspirated engine. The technology of the engine has come so far up that my engine now at 6,000 revs still has torque like the old, normally aspirated engine. The turbo lag nearly doesn't exist. In 1985, 1986, and 1987, yes, there was lag time, but not in the last few years. We are driving the car as if it is a normally aspirated engine. There is almost no lag at all."

Indy Car racing is one of the few viable major series where its race cars still use turbochargers. Although the turbo has really been neutered with a reduction of boost over the years, the current V-8 turbos can move a car from a standstill to 100mph in just over 4sec, with a top speed of over 240mph. The turbo engine has come a long way, and the torque and powerband have improved significantly.

"It's so driveable for a turbocharged engine," 1990 Indy 500 winner Arie Luyendyk says. "The turbo doesn't come in with a bang anymore. You can feed it in, and it kind of has a gradual grab. Not like the old days where there's nothing, nothing, nothing, and then suddenly—bam—all of the sudden, it just takes off [and] goes like that.

"Turbo lag is a big deal in all of the turbo cars. The less turbo lag you have, the better everything is. It is a bit unnatural to drive a car with a lot of turbo lag, because you have to stand on the gas going into the corner in order for you to have any kind of boost for the exit. You do have to adapt to it, is all."

Luyendyk is speaking generally when he talks of boost. Indy Cars don't have the problems that most turbocharged race cars have. Not only are they more efficient than most current turbos, they also have less boost to deal with anyway. The cars drive more like ordinary, normally aspirated—or atmospheric—cars.

Plumbing in the car also helps. Between the intake manifold and the turbo is an area that is very crucial to engineers since that is generally where the pop-off valve was located. For at least two seasons—in 1992 and 1993—it was a major area of experimentation as teams injected fuel, which changed the flow of the air/fuel mix area, to optimize it through the engine. There were two results: First, the injection further cooled the intake, which may have heated up due to the turbulence at the top of the manifold. But as it cooled with the addition of the raw methanol, it created a negative pressure, which, if positioned correctly between the turbo and the plenum, could actually fool the pop-off valve into thinking pressure was less than it actually was. Rumor had it that Ford was injecting fuel directly into the turbo, reducing the temperature and increasing the boost, thereby getting 48-49in, instead of the 45in limit. The pop-off valve is now mounted in the middle of the intake plenum, relative to the position of the engine, so teams are not able to create that low pressure area. Furthermore, teams are no longer allowed to inject fuel anywhere except into the cylinders.

The Future of Turbochargers

What, then, does the future hold for turbo engineers? What could they do to improve the package? "If [turbos] were gone, that would be an improvement," Bain says, again with a smile. "As far as working on the car, that's a really messy part of it. It gets hot, and you have to work the whole package around it. The whole transmission design has to be worked around the turbo. There's a turbo there, and they have to make a space in the bell housing for it to go. Then they have to design where the input shaft is going to go by the turbo, and they have to take into consideration how much heat that thing is making, and they have to keep it away from the gearbox. If you didn't have turbos, the designers would have a whole lot more area to develop different gearboxes. They should, but they probably won't ban them."

He pauses a long moment again to think. "It sure would make my job a lot easier."

Turbos vs. 'Blowers'

The very word "turbo" has become synonymous with power in the modern English language. From Bangor to Bakersfield the word has a special connotation which transcends motoring. Is it good? Is it the best? Then it must be turbo. Or so the thinking goes.

Turbo cars, we might deduce from the colloquialism, are surely the fastest race cars in the world. Yet the answer to the question of whether they truly are is an unequivocal, "it depends."

Turbocharged cars are indeed *some* of the fastest cars on the planet. If supercharged cars were fast, well, turbocharged cars were even better. In fact, the word supercharging and turbocharging are rooted in the same concept. The differences are in *how* power—or the "charge"—is actually delivered.

If you read the rules in many formulae you will discover that the word "supercharged" is often interchanged with "turbocharged." The idea in both cases is exactly the same—to cram as much additional air into the combustion chamber as possible so as to provide more oxygen to burn more fuel and to also raise the compression ratio. The difference between the two processes is how the goal is accomplished. As you know by now, turbos use exhaust gasses to drive the turbine which compresses the air; a supercharger uses a gear or belt drive off the engine's crank to compress the air.

Depending on the type of job at which the engine is expected to excel, the applications will vary greatly. In Top Fuel drag racing, for example, the huge "blowers" mounted on the top of those massive 500ci nitromethane-powered engines have a life expectancy of only a few moments. Total time of use before the engine is torn down and rebuilt is only about 3 minutes—and only about 5 seconds of that is actually at peak power. The engine still craves the air, but it needs it now, not when boost builds—even if it will build in .10 second. The Top Fuel dragster, with its nitro fuel and supercharger, is capable of producing 5,000 horsepower. *Right now.*

The Indy Car, on the other hand, doesn't need all the huge hooded plenum chambers and instantaneous power. As long as it is available in a few fractions of a second, it will do the job just fine. Nowadays, most racing turbos are limited, as is the case at Indy. And at those places where they are not restricted, they are banned outright. The reason is simple: with the right technology, turbos truly can develop unlimited power.

In the late eighties, Formula One cars were capable of producing perhaps 2,000hp for very brief periods of time (such as qualifying)—quite astounding when you consider that power was being produced by a 1.5 liter engine.

Since Indy Cars are equipped with engines almost twice that size, it would seem likely that Indy cars would be faster and more powerful than their counterparts in Europe. But it is not so.

Rules restrict Indy Cars in the amount of boost they can use—about 45 inches. With boost restricted, the car is effectively neutered; with unlimited boost, however, power is only restricted by the internal strength of the engines and the amount of pressure an engineer can design into his engine. The limit is almost boundless.

The supercharger—or, let's call it the mechanical version of the turbo—would sap too much power in a restricted form such as the Indy Car engine. It is less taxing on the engine to use the exhaust gases (as in the case of the turbo) to spin the compressor than to run yet another pump off the crank. In unrestricted form, it is also more difficult to get the nearly unlimited power out of a supercharger. The supercharger gears would actually have to have a gearing which would then need to be changed during operation to compress air at a faster rate as the engine needs it. In turbo cars, the drivers simply turn up the boost—kind of like switch to high gear.

It doesn't really matter. Turbos are out, banned in Europe and relentlessly restricted in Indy Cars. In fact, most production cars have higher boost than most race cars. In Top Fuel, the application of more power is always attractive. And there are no limits to the amount of boost the supercharger can develop, but changing gears on a supercharger is not something a driver supervising a 300mph run has time to do.

For now, super—as in a Top Fueler's supercharger—is defined as excellent.

Chapter 6

Black Magic: The Electronics

Generally, innovation in racing filters down into street car applications. Mechanical gizmos such as turbos, variable timing, active suspension, and rear spoilers are all innovations that have proven to be essential to race cars and have eventually found their way onto street-going vehicles. The trend is usually "Win on Sunday, sell on Monday."

But in the world of electronics, where the consumer goes for the bells and whistles far quicker than the pragmatic race car driver, many of the gains have

Writing letters to "My Mother the Car." Data is being downloaded from the onboard computer to the laptop. The information gathered will be the source of changes for this weekend's race as well as changes at future races.

been offshoots of the automotive industry.

Such systems as digital dashboards, which graphically displayed miles per hour, oil temperature, and rpm, appeared on Cadillacs in the late-seventies. And computers, which recorded and, at the touch of a button, displayed your average fuel mileage, distance that can be traveled on available fuel, and average miles per hour, were available in Lincoln Town Cars in the early-eighties. Comfort and convenience features—or, let's face it, virtually nonessential information systems for street cars—eventually found a permanent home in race cars. Drivers and teams found they couldn't do without them. And as in a street car, what's in the cockpit only begins to tell the story of what's on the car. So under the race car's equivalent of the hood—beneath the sidepod covers, usually on the right-hand side of the car—lurk several ominous-looking, high-tech black boxes.

The whole system is called Electronic Control Management (ECM). It makes everything work, except the radio and the on-board camera. (More about those in a minute.) The ECM's most essential component is the Electronic Control Unit (ECU). This is the one that gets changed the most, and which is commonly known as the black box. It processes all the data from the engine systems, fuel systems, and intake systems and sends that information to the engine. A second box, the spark control box, communicates with the alternator, distributor, and spark plugs. An alternator control box takes information from the ECM to the alternator. A fourth box controls the instrumentation, and another controls the dash and projects information received from the ECU onto the dashboard for the driver to read. That's where all the telemetry comes from.

There are a number of possible assignments for any of the given modules. Depending on what is put into a module, it can accept or record information from chassis to the engine and from cockpit to paddock.

The ECU: The Original Black Box

Back to the ECU, the *original* black box. New materials and electronics have advanced the technology of the Indy Car a quantum distance in the last six to eight years. That jump came in the form of improved performance. The engines, too, have changed considerably, but more importantly, designers and team personnel can now see exactly what's happening inside the power plant. No more fussing with plugs to determine how the mixture is burning; no more trying to determine the throttle application out of any given corner. The computer does it all. There is no hiding from it either.

Emerson Fittipaldi says, "We can see exactly what's going on. We can see what's going on when the car is running or after it's been shut down. It's the best. Like, for example, this morning, coming out of slow corners, I had a type of misfiring out of the hair-

pins between 5,000 and 6,000 revs. I went to the Chevrolet people to see the trace, and it was a little lean in both situations, and they immediately changed the fuel map."

The map. Drivers constantly talk about this map, but what is it? They are referring to the computer mapping of fuel and air ratios for the different rpm ranges and what happens when those ratios change. Added into that equation is the amount of power being made at different rpm ranges. So the maps—which the engineers can see on their computer screens as graphs—will be different for every track. The altitudes of the track play an important role in the calculations. That is, the altitudes above sea level and as well as the changes in track altitude. The atmospheric pressure, air density, and humidity are all factors. Such parameters can change dramatically on any given day, and the maps contain directions out of the quandary. Mapping is all done in the ECU.

For each race weekend, the ECU, or the entire system, is returned to the engine manufacturer so that the appropriate set of criteria can be entered into the unit. Both Ilmor—and Ford have their own systems and have software that is configured specifically

The black boxes, which pretty much control the entire operation of the car. The system is called the electronic control management (ECM), which is broke into several units. The first is the ECU—the electronic control unit that takes all the data from the engine systems, fuel systems, and intake systems and sends it to the engine. Next there is the spark control box, which talks to the alternator, distributor, and spark plugs. Then there's an alternator control box, which takes information from the engine management box to the alternator. Another black box controls the instrumentation. Another box specifically feeds information to the dash, and as information is received from the ECU, it translates it to provide what is eventually read on the dashboard by the driver.

Under the sidepod covering—wherever it fits, the electrical system is mounted as if it is an afterthought, yet it does one of the most significant jobs of any component on the car.

The dash holds a great deal of information. The dash in today's Indy Cars is now all digital. Since the cars travel at 240mph and a mile is gobbled up every 15 seconds, the driver doesn't have time to glance down, determine where the needle is in relation to the gauge, and process the information. He needs it now. Graphic displays of performance data immediately compute in his brain.

for each particular track. That doesn't mean the engine run specifically from that software, but the software is the engine's guideline. The engine constantly monitors specific areas that are determined by the software.

"I think the whole thing has improved," Fittipaldi says. "The engine has improved, but the electronics have made a big step ahead to react quicker. I mean, we are getting much more revs than we used to. A lot of this has to do with the monitoring and the new materials in the valve springs and things."

It's safe to say that the gains in the engine have come more rapidly since the engine has been so efficiently quantified.

At the same time, the engine-monitoring software will tell you things about other areas of the car as well. Teams can put sensors on the shocks to determine what the shocks are doing and on the wheels to see how much they are being worked and whether the rates need to be changed. They can monitor the brakes for temperature readings. Also available are sensors that look at the ground and tell the team what the ride height is, as well as sensors that determine the steering input.

This enables the team to literally map the course so that they can pick a certain corner that on any particular lap they can deduce how far the wheel was turned and how close to the ground the bottom of the tub was. They can then compare it to other corners and other laps, again and again.

This is all strictly informational. The suspension, the engine, and any other devices on the car are *not* adjustable via telemetry. It is only data acquisition, and it is up to the driver to change the fuel mixture, change the boost, control the sway bars, and adjust the shocks.

Forms of Telemetry

There are three different types of telemetry. The basic system reads the information while the car is on the racetrack. It relays the information when the driver brings the car back into the pits and plugs it into a terminal. Most teams use what's called the Pi system, a brand name that has now become an almost generic term. The next step up is a system of telemetry that transmits to the driver's pitside system once a lap.

The tachometer, fuel pressure, fuel mileage, boost, and fuel mix are all monitored, even at speeds of up to 240 mph. Warning lights alert a driver to critical levels of fuel and critical operating temperatures. The low fuel level can be remedied with a pit stop. High temperatures—those high enough to trigger warning systems—might be enough to put a driver out of a race.

The small antenna on each side of the nosecone transmit the telemetry messages from the car to the pit. The ECU translates information to the pits there via a number of assignments. Crews will adjust the car based on what comes over the air from cockpit to paddock. This antenna setup is from the old Truesports car. More common today is to see the antenna sticking straight up out of the bodywork at the nose of the car.

And then there's real-time telemetry, which is transmitted via a radio dedicated solely to telemetry and is constantly in use while the car is driving around the track. Although the driver won't see what's going on by looking at his dash, the team will usually keep him informed.

As in the Cadillac, the dash on a modern Indy Car is now all digital. But in this case, form follows function. For the 65-year-old Coupe de Ville driver, the digital dash was simply a novelty; at 55mph, there was plenty of time to look at an analog gauge. But in

The radio is operated via a button off the steering wheel; a driver depresses the button to speak to the pits. "I can't see how NASA can talk to satellites that are on the other end of the solar system when we can't even seem to get our radios to work with a car that's just on the other side of the racetrack," said one crewman. "That's probably a matter of throwing more money at it I guess. They seem to be really temperamental things. They've made a lot of improvements, though." The radio feeds are actually going to "ears" all over the track. These days it's common for race fans to monitor conversations between cars and pits. For some big events, monitors can be leased at the race site, and transmission frequencies for individual teams are common knowledge on the circuit. Thus, competing teams can tune in on each other's fueling and tire changing plans. From time to time, teams change the frequencies on which they communicating to try to find more privacy.

The gigantic antenna at the other end of the transmission is in the pits and it monitors two or three types of telemetry: a basic system reads the information while the car is on the racetrack and spits back the information when the driver brings it back into the pits; the second type is "real time" telemetry which is dedicated via radio solely to telemetry and is constantly being used while the car is driving around the track, updating the crew every second; the last style updates the pit computer once a lap—usually as the driver passes start/finish.

Indy Cars, where the cars travel at 240mph and a mile is gobbled up every 15sec (in Top Fuel terms, that's four successive quarter-miles at 3.75sec each), the driver doesn't have time to glance down, determine where the needle is in relation to the gauge, and process the information. He needs the information *now*, and a graphic display is the answer. If, say, at the exit of Laguna Seca's Corkscrew, he can glance down and see a change in rpm, he'll know his gain immediately. Back at the pits, through the telemetry, the crew will know what he did to get the extra speed, and they can then process the information to make it easier for him to repeat his performance the next time he goes out to practice.

Crews have had to go back to school to figure out what's happening on their cars. The changes for the driver have been incremental. The advantages of the digital system are fairly obvious—especially the ability to relay information from the car to the pits and straight to the viewer so the driver doesn't have to tell the crew what's going on as he's trying to keep the race car going along at full clip. But for mechanics, complications of the new technology have become a major source of frustration. Not that it doesn't work; not that it isn't critical. It's just complicated.

According to Emerson Fittipaldi, thanks to telemetry and electrical monitoring systems, "We can see exactly what's going on. We can see what's going on when the car is running or after it's been shut down." It's the best. For example, this morning, coming out of slow corners I had a type of misfiring out of the hairpins between five and six thousand revs. I went to the Chevrolet people to see the trace and it was a little lean on both situations and they immediately changed the fuel map."

"When I started in 1985, they didn't have any control systems," mechanic Randy Bain says. "It was all mechanically done. There was the distributor, the alternator, the battery, and basically that was it. There wasn't any electronic fuel control; that was all done with a mechanical pump. What the electronics has allowed them to do is to monitor a whole bunch of different systems so that [the car] can be more precisely controlled. There has been a gain in performance—in horsepower—but mostly what they've gained is [the ability to make] the engine run more efficiently."

Then Bain was quiet, trying to espouse the spirit of the contemporary system. Eventually he says with refreshing candor, "It makes my life miserable. First of all, you have to make the thing work. That's pretty much the hardest part. You have to get a mechanical potentiometer to read it electronically, so that means something else that has to be bolted on the car. Not only does it have to be bolted on, but it has to be calibrated. You have to confirm that it's all working and chances are that one of them will fail. It's one of those Catch-22 deals: You can probably run just as fast without it, but since it's available, you have to have it so that you don't lose ground."

If there's one thing the team can take heart in, it's the fact that drivers can no longer blame the car for their mistakes. Even crews that have excellent relationships with their drivers are happy to know that the driver has to face the music every time he steps out of the car. If the throttle application is 100 percent, he has done his job. If it isn't, he can't possibly blame the car.

Telemetry has become a classic way of determining whether the driver is really as fearless as he thinks he is. In the past, the team took for granted that he was going flat out all the time. Now, the driver's story can be corroborated or refuted.

"The classic story is about the driver who says he's flat through the whole track and the car won't go any faster," says Bain. "So you look at the computer, and it says he's [at] 92 percent throttle going into turn three. You have flat, you have really flat, and you have flat-flat. If the driver says he's flat, it's not always

The entire system is returned to the manufacturer prior to each race so the appropriate set of criteria can be entered into the unit. Both Ilmor and Ford have their own systems with a pre-determined piece of software that is configured for each particular track. The software is the engine guideline and the engine constantly monitors specific areas that are determined by the software.

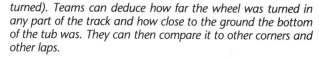

The software will tell teams things about the shocks; they can put sensors on the wheels to see if the rates need to be changed; they can monitor the brakes for temperature readings; ride height; and steering input (the amount that it's

turned). Teams can deduce how far the wheel was turned in any part of the track and how close to the ground the bottom of the tub was. They can then compare it to other corners and other laps.

The telemetry is all strictly informational. The suspension, the engine, and any other devices on the car is not adjustable via telemetry. The system provides only for data acquisition and the only things the driver can actually do is to change the fuel mixture, change the boost, control the sway bars, and adjust the shocks.

the case. He'll say the boost says one thing, but he only looks at it on the straight-aways and it may be going way down in the turns."

Goal #1: Communications

The primary focus of the electronics package has become communication—whether from the driver's throttle foot to the pits or from his mouth to the transporter or from the front of the car to the television cameras that carry the signal all over the world. There seem to be more and more wires and electronic hookups now than ever before.

Most, like the radio, are self-contained, using their own batteries and generating their own power. The radio is only important when it doesn't work (which is quite often, according to most crews), forcing crews to go back to the time-honored system of hand signals and pit boards. Even when the radio does work properly, it can operate on only a few frequencies. Furthermore, when one part of the system fails, it all fails—and that can be quite costly, considering that radios cost about $1,500. A single mechanic has to understand what may have failed in the radio and fix it.

"I can't see how NASA can talk to satellites that are on the other end of the solar system when we can't even seem to get our radios to work with a car that's just on the other side of the racetrack," Bain says. "That's probably a matter of throwing more money at it, I guess. They seem to be really temperamental things. They've made a lot of improvements, though."

Radios, which have been used for quite a few years longer than in-car television cameras, don't seem to be fail-safe. In contrast, complicated television cameras have surprisingly reliability records. Just a few years ago, the only way to take pictures of a car at speed were with a normal, commercial-quality camera mounted on the top of the car. This obviously was not going to work during a race—which meant that until about 1987, race fans were only able to watch qualifying. It was then that a few astute television people discovered a way to make the cameras lighter and portable.

The camera itself is about the size of a cigarette. The small wing mounted over the driver's right shoulder is the camera unit, but most of that package is the apparatus that moves the lens screen. The entire package—the wires, boxes, batteries, lens, and roll of clear plastic film that keeps the view clear—weighs 5 to 6lb. Cameras are here to stay, so much so that Lola

The small button-looking device on Andretti's car is a camera which looks backward at the field behind his car. The camera itself is small enough, but the battery takes up some room. Nevertheless, the cameras are usually more reliable than other much more critical gadgetry. Cameras looking forward are commonly mounted on the right side of the roll bar, and are roughly the size of a roll-on deodorant container. Again, it's the camera housing, battery, and lens roll-off mechanism that takes up most of the space; the camera itself is remarkably small. In the modern world of sponsor exposure, television viewers see numerous sponsor logos on the car's bodywork each time an in-car camera view is shown.

Timing and scoring creates one more set of wires, batteries, and screens as the cars are fitted with new computers which send signals as they cross the start-finish line, scoring the car immediately.

many are cast by using a metal matrix technique of quenching and cooling that imbues the piece with the strength of a billeted piece of metal without having to compromise the overall design to accommodate machining. Pistons are constructed with small holes to catch air so that they're constantly being cooled as the car slices through the air. Not only does the airflow between the disc and the piston or pad cool the caliper, the piston helps cool them as well. The drilled pistons also become lighter.

Average calipers cost $1,500 to $2,500 each, and metal matrix aluminum units can cost up to $4,000. Pads cost from $100 per axle set (two wheels only) for the economy version to $400 per axle set for imported carbon metal style.

Discs Absorb the Heat, Get Pitched

Discs, however, are a different component. They are neither reliable nor resilient. They generally last less than a weekend and then have to be scrapped. The extreme heat on the rotors or discs makes them a very weak link in the chain.

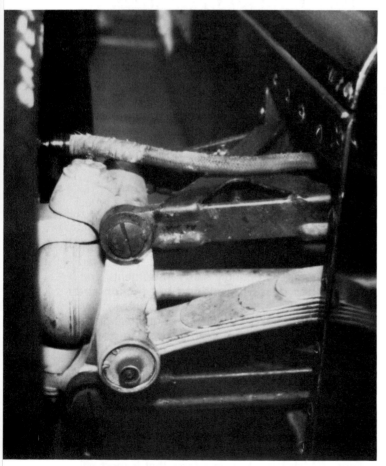

Hydraulic brakes on Louie Meyer's 1936 Miller-Stevens Indy 500 winner. The units were prone to overheating and both bad fade and malfunction. Thankfully, they were not used often in an oval track race. Ray Touriel

State-of-the-art discs on Indy Cars are, oddly, very similar to those on the average passenger car and are made of regular cast-iron. There are different additives, such as materials that help the iron withstand extreme heat cycles and hardness enhancers. Average discs cost $170-$200; higher-quality imports cost $400-$450.

The material may be fairly low-tech, but the machining is not. All are matched to close tolerances. Three- to four-thousandths of an inch (.003-.004in) will throw the discs off and make them virtually undriveable. That is, three- to four-thousandths of sideways change. Although the horizontal, or lateral—also called run-out—tolerances are tight, the discs expand. The diameter changes fairly radically. The discs usually have 13in diameters, but under heavy braking, that increases to about 13.08in, an eighty-one-thousandths change.

Teams will use two car sets of brakes per weekend—two sets of pads and two sets of discs. Watching them glow red-hot as the cars slow from high-speed straight-aways to slow hairpins, one can understand why.

"The most consumable part of the car are the brake discs and pads," explains Brembo representative Mark Cornwell. "[They see] more energy than just about any other part of the car except maybe the gearbox. It's a friction component. And any types of metal will have a limited life expectancy. They go up to between 1200 and 1400deg very quickly."

If the caliper gets above 450deg Fahrenheit (200deg Centigrade), the fluid will boil. Calipers heat up and cool down slowly unlike discs, which can go from about 400deg on the straight-away to 1200deg in a corner in fewer than 1sec.

A few years ago, the uprights and certain components of a handful of cars were not designed quite right. Fluid boiled. Drivers did what they could to preserve the brakes, saving the car for the end. The uprights have been redesigned and improved perhaps 40 percent and the focus has changed. Discs are now expected to wear out. The drivers who at one time saved their brakes to prevent boiling can now jump on them with all their might.

The distance from the master cylinder to the rear calipers is significant: room enough for another set of brakes. "It's a volume thing," says Cornwell. "The system itself has very little brake fluid in it really. When the pads are new, you have very little fluid in the system. All it does when it boils is take that little bit of fluid and make it into a vapor. That vapor is compressible, and it makes for a soft pedal."

A soft pedal is devastating to the driver because he loses confidence in the brakes and doesn't know how deep he can go into a corner. He has to know exactly what the limits are. But due to both suspension changes as well as better ducting, fluid boiling is not the problem it was, and drivers now worry less about stopping power.

Miller's drum brakes off a "91." These look like aluminum knockoffs fabricated later. Miller's were nickle plated, the shoes cast aluminum with brass-wire impregnated filler material and the hubs were machined from a solid billet. The front brakes *(seen here) were actuated by hand lever; the rears by foot pedal. They only weighed about nine pounds each—very light for those days—and were strictly racing brakes good only for a few pit stops and nothing else. Ray Touriel*

Disc temperatures are monitored by a series of heat-immune paints—at least immune to a point. When the paint burns off, the crew knows the brake has heated past its immunity point. If the paint is not burned or radically discolored, the brakes are cooling too much. Green paint generally burns away at 430deg Centigrade, orange at 540deg Centigrade, and red at 610deg Centigrade. The caliper would be a different shape altogether if it reached these temperatures, so thermal stickers are used to gauge them.

Formula One cars, with their carbon fiber discs and pads, can stop on a dime; Indy Car brakes, which are cast-iron and carbon-metallic pads cannot stop nearly as quickly. Perhaps in a race between an Indy Car and a Grand Prix car, the Grand Prix car would stop much faster and the advantage would be enough to win the race.

Measuring Their Braking Power

Just how fast do Indy Cars stop?

If a production-based car with street tires can get

Perhaps the most ignored suggestion in racing. Its is unclear whether this brake light was deliberately left in place for racing, or whether the car was driven once as a street car. Curious component on a race car, either way. Ray Touriel

While a production car with street tires can get as high as 1.3 negative Gs, an Indy Car—at top speed—can produce about 3.5 negative Gs. That's a lot of inertia, a lot of force and speed to try to rein in for a driver can make it around a sharp turn in the midst of traffic. The brake calipers are coolest at top speed, the down force is greatest, and the initial stopping ability is the most powerful.

as high as, say, 1 G, or maybe 1.3 negative Gs, an Indy Car at top speed can produce as much as 3.5 negative Gs. The qualifying statement "top speed" is important because the brakes are most efficient when the car is at top speed. The calipers are coolest, the down force is greatest, and the initial stopping ability is the most powerful. As the car slows, these factors change. The caliper heats, the tires reach their limits, down force is reduced, and the G forces ease up. Formula One cars can produce more than 4 negative Gs simply because they can still use carbon fiber.

"Carbon fiber brakes heat up in a split second to 600+deg. Instant retardation. They're much lighter, so they don't need the energy to stop," Nigel Mansell comments. "I would say they have twice the braking power than what we have with these current [Indy] cars. Plus the Formula One car is 500lb lighter, so it has even more braking power since it's not stopping such a heavy car. These steel brakes are very, very good; you just have to brake a little earlier, and they're a bit less predictable [at] certain periods of

time because the window of temperature is sort of greater and smaller at the same time. [T]hey work, [but] they are obviously not as efficient."

Carbon fiber brakes react similarly to cast-iron discs. Both materials disperse heat, but carbon fiber quickly assimilates the heat and radiates it through the piece. Also, cast-iron doesn't glow as easily.

There are currently two major carbon fiber brake makers. One manufactures its brakes so that the friction surfaces take most of the heat, producing flashes of red. The other radiates the heat throughout the piece of carbon fiber and does not glow quite as red. Also, the carbon disc can withstand close to 1800deg Fahrenheit heat.

So why don't Indy Cars use carbon fiber? They did, but CART decided that small, lower-budget teams had a difficult time staying competitive with bigger teams that could afford carbon fiber. At the same time, the cars were reaching speeds that were just a bit higher than officials wanted to see. So the CART Board of Directors banned carbon fiber brakes.

Tuning the Brakes

There are only a few ways to tune the brakes in the paddock during race weekend.

"If you've got a circuit that is really hard on brakes at a place that is a fairly slow track where you get a lot of heat, you'll probably improve the ducting," says Cornwell. "You'll improve the brake duct to try to get in more air and cool the brakes. You can't let the brakes get too hot [or] they will boil the fluid and [will] get air in the system, and you'll lose the brake pedal. You can't have any air in your system, or you obviously [will] bleed the brakes. You'll try and scoop more air in not only to cool the rotor, but also [to] cool the caliper, which in turn tries to cool the pads."

"You have differing brake rotors that you can put on, different brake pads you can put on, different brake scoops you can put on. All of those are affected by the circuit and by the driver. Some drivers are harder on brakes than others. You have to have the proper size brakes to get cooling." He pauses for a minute to think. "You don't want them too cool. Carbon metallic brakes pads work better with some heat in them. So you can't get them too cool, but you have to get them hot enough to work—again, not so hot that they're going to break the brake rotor or crack or fracture the brake rotor. It's really a difficult, touchy situation."

The obvious consequences of a failed brake could be disastrous. Imagine going into Long Beach's first corner at 170mph and experiencing a brake failure. Drivers are sensitive to that pedal in the middle of the pedal assembly. It is what keeps them alive.

"Any brake failure could be disastrous," echoes Arie Luyendyk. "I'm more gentle on brakes than, say, Eddie Cheever is. The brake pad technology has come along a long way. We're not allowed to have carbon

Nigel Mansell had to get used to the difference between the carbon fiber brakes that stopped on a dime and the cast iron brakes that stop, well, on a quarter. Formula One cars get up over four negative Gs simply because they can still use carbon fiber. "Carbon fiber brakes heat up in a split second to 600-plus degrees," Mansell says. "Instant retardation. They're much lighter so they don't need the energy to stop. I would say they have twice the braking power than what we have with these current [Indy] cars. Plus the Formula One car is 500lb lighter so it has even more braking power since it's not stopping such a heavy car. These steel brakes are very, very good; you just have to brake a little earlier and they're a bit less predictable at certain periods of time at temperature because the window of temperature is sort of greater and smaller at the same time, and they are obviously not as efficient.

Carbon fiber may not be allowed on Indy Car discs, but it is fairly common on the duct work. The duct work has to be designed so it provides some cooling air flow without sticking out into the air to much itself.

fiber brakes, but we do have a brake pad that does have a lot of carbon incorporated into it: carbon and brass and asbestos and copper. The worst set of circumstances is a complete failure of the system. Air in the system.," Luyendyk shakes his head. "It happens where all [of a] sudden, there's no brake pedal there.

"The brakes have come a long way, and a lot of that has to do with the pads. The discs are ventilated, so the cars have pretty nice, big cooling ducts on them so we can use them to cool them off pretty good. And they're prebedded and preheated."

At one time, drivers had to bed the brakes so that as the heat cycles were applied, the heat drew out the

chemicals, resins, and gasses to actually cure the pads. Manufacturers now offer race-ready pads. Most carbon metallic pads do not have to be run before use, although many drivers do bed them anyway, just for personal comfort. They want to make sure there is nothing wrong with the brakes before they launch into a race.

In the final analysis, brakes are still one of the few pieces of equipment in the car that the driver has a great deal of control over. He can save the brakes, or he can abuse them, forcing fade or, in a worst-case scenario, a complete failure. The team can give him an edge, but the driver, with his control over the equipment, will ultimately make the difference.

"It's a little bit of driving technique and a little bit of self-preservation—or equipment preservation," says Danny Sullivan. "A lot of guys keep their left foot brake and they tend to drag their foot. I'm probably lighter on them than anybody else."

So they all say.

Chapter 8

Kept in Suspension: The Suspension

In 1923, Fred Duesenberg produced a report for the Society of Automotive Engineers (SAE) which studied the effects of lightening unsprung weight on a race car. He reported that by reducing the rear axle weight by less than 50lb, he could gain 10mph on a bumpy track.

If the effects of unsprung weight could improve performance by minimizing the effects of the wheels hopping, it was obvious to see what damping the movement of the wheel—which was weighing less and less over time—could do.

The first dampers were lever-type units that worked via friction resistance. Damping could be increased or decreased by tightening or loosening the clamping force on the levers. Although it wasn't an on-off type of system, it always operated with little or no fine-tuning.

By the late-twenties, hydraulic shocks gave much better tuning with almost infinite adjustments, as well as much smoother damping. The most popular unit was bulky but effective with a piston engaged by the movement of a rod that turned as the wheel moved up and pushed the piston, forcing the fluid down and thwarting the movement of the wheel. The shocks could be adjusted easily by changing a set of springs and fluid jets.

As frames went from ladder-type in the forties to tube-type space frames in the fifties, they became more of a predictable commodity. The frame no longer twisted and flexed like an old stepladder. With one side of the handling equation more or less nailed down, the other facets quickly developed.

A stiffer frame helped the front wheels bite. Reducing the frame's twist kept the front wheels on the ground better. That, added to a general lightening of unsprung weight and improved damping, increased overall performance a great deal, and speeds rose.

The advent of the magnesium wheel also helped enormously. The old Rudge-type wire wheels were developed to be light and flexible to be a damper of sorts. With the hydraulic shocks and limited twist of the new chassis, the last thing the new cars needed was a wheel that flexed. It was also, by standards of the day, too heavy. Ted Halibrand cast a magnesium disc wheel that was both strong and rigid. Within a few seasons, this wheel completely replaced wire ones.

At the same time, Monroe developed a telescopic tube that aided damping. The old lever hydraulic shocks were bulky and too complex. Tube shocks were easier to install, service, replace, and understand. As part of its advertising campaign, Monroe supplied several Indy race cars with telescopic shocks. It was inexpensive genius—quickly, all teams used the telescopic shock.

Two major trends in suspension continue to this day. First, there has been a tendency to move as much of the suspension as possible inboard, away from the airstream. In older cars, the springs, shocks, uprights, and all wishbones are mounted in such a way that they create a gigantic amount of drag. Open-wheeled cars already have too much drag; eliminating as much of it as possible has been the goal for the past fifteen years.

Second, there has been a trend toward quick adjustability. Of the three components that enhance or reduce the adhesion capacity of the car—tires, aerodynamic down force, and suspension—suspension has always been the most complicated to change. Designers strive to simplify it and make it adjustable.

The Front Suspension

So what is that mass of black tubing and other stuff that looks like dried linguini? Sit back and hold on. The front suspension consists of a rocker connected to part of the upright, or hub. The rocker is exactly what its name implies: a simple, mechanical piece that moves—or rocks—when pressure is applied, thereby applying force to the shock or damper. There is an upper wishbone and a lower wishbone, both of which are essentially just tubing that runs from the

Made with high strength, usually solid, rod material, this de Dion type front axle was standard equipment for most race cars of the twenties and thirties. It would be the mid thirties *before independent suspension was successfully integrated and longer before it was common. Ray Touriel*

car's body to the upright. Each is shaped like a wishbone or an elongated "V."

The pushrods run diagonally from the bottom wishbone, which makes up the bottom part of the upright where the wheel is bolted, up to the rocker. The rocker has a pivot point, thereby actuating the bottom of the shock.

So again, when the wishbone and upright go up and down as the car travels over bumps or corners, the wheel pushes the pushrod, activating the rocker, which compresses the damper. The damper has a spring so that the wheel has both compression and rebound. The spring is the rebound and the damper eases the movement. Both rebound and the car's ride height are controlled with the spring rate on top of the damper.

Also mounted to the rocker and moving up with the shock as it is actuated is a 2ft-long anti-roll bar link, which keeps the car from reacting like a street car. For example, as the right wheel hits a bump in the road, the wheel moves up. As it does, it applies the rocker, which actuates the shock and pulls on the anti-roll bar link. Think of the link as one part of

This shock absorber is a variation of common types of the early thirties. The leaf springs were mounted transversely and kept the suspension tight and the wheels connected with the road. The shock dampened the movement via a mechanical spring-type device which offered resistance via friction. A breed of similar devices appeared which were damped via hydraulics. Tube shocks would not appear until around 1950. Ray Touriel

The linguini called an Indy Car front suspension consists of a rocker which moves—or rocks—as the wheel does, thereby applying as force to the shock or damper. The pushrods run diagonally from the bottom wishbone, which makes up the bottom part of the upright where the wheel is bolted, and runs up to the rocker. The rocker has a pivot point which actuates the bottom of the shock.

a U. The long arms of the U are the links and the curve is the anti-roll bar. So the shock wants to go up, but it can't because it is tied to the bottom of the U. To throw a monkey wrench into this mess, remember that the U is also attached to the other wheel. So it abates the pushrod, as well as the wheel attached to the other end, from moving any farther. At the end of the link—at the bottom of the U—is what looks like a set of short, thin bicycle forks, with a solid bar joining them together just below the driver's feet. Think of these forks as the areas of the U's curve. They control the anti-roll bar. The blades of the two-pronged fork can be turned and tuned. On an oval, the teams would turn the thin side in, creating stiff resistance and making it necessary for the bar to twist. On most road courses, they would swivel so that the pliable sides are facing the shocks—in other words, giving the roll bar some slack. For the most part, the tuning of the suspension comes from this apparatus.

The Rear Suspension

The rear suspension consists of a rocker suspension that acts as a type of a bell crank. There is one pivot point—where the shock and the pushrod mount. Think of a segmented broom handle mounted horizontally on the top of the transmission at the pivot point. Imagine there is a steel bar through the entire length of the piece that allows some pieces to move around on the axis, while other pieces are secured to the tranny. Instead of the shocks being mounted at the top of the assembly and perpendicular to the pushrods, they are mounted almost parallel to the pushrods and drop slightly below the rockers.

Mounting holes change the ratio of a rocker to indicate whether it's a linear rate rocker or a rising rate

The rockers, which push the end of the shock as the wheels move up, which compresses the damper. The wheel has both compression and rebound, with the spring being the rebound and the damper eases the movement. You can control the rebound with the spring rate on top of the damper. It also con- *trols the car's ride height. As the shock moves up, it pulls the tie-rod which tugs at the anti-roll bar. From this photo you should be able to see the tips of the "bicycle forks," which can be turned on their axis to become stiffer or softer, depending on the track.*

rocker. There is a toe link and an upper and lower wishbone. The pushrod is connected to the rocker. Take what you know about the front suspension and move it to the back. In other words, you have a set of rockers, a set of pushrods, four wishbones, and an anti-roll bar with the fork setup (the half shafts are in the middle to power the car). It is configured differently, but the pieces are almost exactly the same. The pickup points are right off the gearbox and, oddly, the anti-roll bar goes straight through the gearbox.

Back to the shocks. Linear rate is basically a one-to-one rocker ratio. By whatever increment a shock moves, it is compensated by an exact equal movement of the pushrod; if it moves 1in, the pushrod moves 1in. Depending on the rate, with the rising rate rocker, the shock will move a lot more than the pushrod. The shocks and assembly can change the car's ride height. By adjusting the shock up and down in its housing, the car's suspension changes and the clearance increases or decreases. The other way to change the ride height is to move the pushrod up or down by means of an adjustable thread at the end of the tubing. By undoing the jam nut, an adjustment nut can be moved, which effectively lengthens or shortens the pushrod. One-sixth of a turn of that nut can make a big difference in ride height.

How the Suspensions Really Work

Let's look at how the suspensions can be adjusted. As an example, if the driver has a small power understeer problem—that is, if he's going through a small corner and it pushes to the outside of the corner when he puts the throttle down—the team will put some anti-squat on the rear of the car by changing the angles of the upper and lower wishbone legs. The geometry mix will fix it by keeping the rear of the car from squatting down as power is applied. There's no difference in a passenger car. When the driver applies power, the rear of the car wants to sink and the front of the car comes up, creating a less-efficient tire patch and ultimately causing understeer. Street car manufacturers design anti-squat into the suspension: the

Strong but light, aero tubing helps reduce the car's drag, yet crew men can actually stand on it. It is relatively aerodynamic stuff as well.

front leg of the upper and lower wishbone will be higher than the rear leg. That will help keep the car from squatting under power, which will then make the front end stick more effectively.

Amazingly, on the 1993 Lola, the front rockers are mounted right to the carbon fiber tub. They are bolted to that mount with a top boss that's bolted and glued to the chassis. It's an incredibly strong assembly. The linguini—the pieces of tubing—are made of 4130 aerotubing. The tubes are slightly crushed so that air moves around them more efficiently.

The cars are very stiff from nose to tail. Roll stiffness is a characteristic that engineers strive to achieve. Basically, designers look at the car as having five springs: the four individual suspension pieces of the car, plus the flex of the car itself. They try to eliminate that fifth spring as much as possible. Perhaps you've seen the results of the process: When an Indy Car gets a flat tire, it will lift the opposite corner up in the air.

In a race, a suspension team is divided and given specific duties, usually with one man up front in charge of all the front suspension components, one in the rear in charge of all the rear components, and one

who integrates what's happening in the front with what's going on in the back.

Depending on the types of circuit—road courses or ovals—the team is also responsible for making sure the car is prepared properly and is safe to drive. The engineer will give the mechanics a "build sheet" from an engineer back at the shop that specifies what sort of set-up the team will run. With several different types of suspension, the mechanics can put on different roll centers—either a low roll center or a high roll center; they can put anti-squat in the front or the rear, and anti-dive in the front or anti-squat in the rear. They can run various percentages of each; they can create a car with a high-caster or a low-caster suspension. Different rockers have different ratios. Rising rate rockers are usually used on road courses, and linear ratio rockers are mostly used on ovals. Some drivers swap setups and use either at both type of track.

For example, since Indianapolis is the fastest oval, teams running at Indy will run a long-wheelbase, oval-track configuration at 113in in length, meaning it will have positive camber on the left side and negative camber on the right. Camber is the wheel's rela-

Notice how the wheels are toed in—pigeon toed—on Robbie Buhl's car. On a street car you expect to see the wheels pointed dead ahead while the steering wheel is set straight ahead.

With the wheels toed in, the car will want to automatically go the direction of the track when adjusted correctly.

Al Unser, Jr.'s, Galles gets heavy in the front end under hard braking for Laguna Seca's corkscrew.

Didier Theys' Lola has its wheels slightly cambered, with the tops of the wheels a few degrees closer together than the bottoms. The car tends to be more responsive—but also more difficult to control

Mario Andretti's Newman-Haas is relatively well-balanced while braking for the Corkscrew turns at Laguna Seca. Perhaps that is why the team won championships in 1991 and 1993 and produced a runner-up in 1992.

tionship to the ground; that is, usually you expect to look at a wheel and see it perpendicular to the ground. They will probably use about 1.25deg positive (camber) on the left front and 3.5deg to 3.75deg negative camber in the right front. Camber presupposes it is not at a 90deg angle to the track surface but is perhaps somewhat slanted so that the top of the wheel is farther in toward the center of the car than the bottom.

At Indy, the car will also have very little toe-out in the front, and the wheels will be practically straight. Toe-out is the opposite of toe-in. Toe-in is the front/rear relationship of the wheel and tire. On a street car, you expect to see the wheels pointed dead ahead while the steering wheel is set straight ahead, but toe-in basically pigeon-toes the car, moving the front of the tires (the toes) in toward the middle and the rear of the tires (the heels, to use the same analogy) out. To toe the car changes its attitude. The car will want to automatically go the direction of the track when adjusted correctly. Remember the time you ran over the curb and the car refused to track cor-

Sorted, stacked and ready, these springs will be lugged to each race until the team discovers they are redundant. Only then will they be removed from inventory. Some will never be used.

Decisions, decisions. The driver will give the crew an idea of whether he wants linear or rising rate damping. The damping is aided by spring selection. Linear rate is basically a one-to-one rocker ratio, meaning whatever increment shock moves, it is compensated by an exact equal movement of the pushrod. The rising rate rocker will move a lot more than whatever the pushrod moves. Pairs of springs are tied together here so they will be used in matched sets for uniform set-ups.

rectly when you released the steering wheel, perhaps trying to put you in the bushes at the side of the road? Race car engineers try to create that condition deliberately; they just direct the car into the turns rather than into the trees. So the car might have just a little bit toe-out on the front and no toe-out in the left rear. The right rear might be toed-in about sixty- to eighty-thousandths of an inch (.006-.008in). The right rear is toed-in because on super-speedways the driver turns left exclusively, and the right rear will help the car turn. Care must be used on the left rear because if it is toed-out too far, the car will steer itself from the rear, which can induce oversteer.

On the front suspension, the caster is usually 1.5deg. Caster is the amount that the wheel is ahead or behind the axle. Think of an old Harley-Davidson motorcycle, the ones with the huge forks. The amount the wheel moves forward—the elongation—can be considered caster. Caster changes the car's responsiveness; the farther out, the more responsive.

Note the rocker linkage in this photo. As the wheel moves up vertically, the rocker pushes the lower arm in, which activates the spring and damper. The anti-roll bar is attached via a link to the other damper and control arm.

From Ovals to Road Courses

An oval is an oval, and there are few changes from Phoenix to Indianapolis. The biggest differences are going to be between road courses and ovals. For road courses, teams run 111in short-wheelbases (depending on driver input, teams may run a long-wheelbase on a road course). Road course to road course will depend on whether racing is done on an actual permanent circuit or a street circuit. For example, there's a difference between Elkhart Lake, which is a fairly fast, permanent road circuit, and Toronto, which is a short, slow track.

Whether the circuit is tight and slow or long and fast, adjustment depends on what the drivers say the car is doing.

"It's hard to say what you do without hearing what [the driver] has to say what it's doing," Brian Barnhardt of Budweiser King Racing says. "I mean, you go with the base line. You go with what you think the car wants to do. You might run more camber. You'll run more negative camber in both front tires in a street course than you would on a super-fast road course. You have maybe close to 4deg negative camber in both front tires [at], let's say, Long Beach or something. Or you may have 3-3.5deg negative camber in both front tires at Elkhart. At the street course, it would help you turn in quite a bit, and will give you some bite in the front end of the car. It also makes the car extremely darty."

Barnhardt explains that the more camber a car has, the less tire patch actually gets to the ground. That tends to make the car move very quickly, sometimes without the driver wanting it to. So for a high-speed circuit, teams will cut back on the camber. The street courses tend to be quite a bit slower. Their average lap time is 95-110mph. But at a place like Elkhart Lake, where the average lap is close to 140mph, the

Springs are sorted and arranged according to tension. Teams are occasionally forced to change springs in the pits... not a chore the crew looks forward to. Notice the difference in thickness of the spring material.

team has to make special adjustments.

"The toughest course is Elkhart Lake," Barnhardt says, "because there [are] a few slow corners. There are two really fast straight-aways that are up between 190- and 200-mile straight-aways. And at the end of those straight-aways, there's a second-gear corner which is hard on brakes because you go from that fast to fairly slow in [a] short period of time. There is a place in the back that is a long, sweeping corner called the carrousel, that if you can get through the kink in the carrousel flat, you've got the car set up really well. If you [have] to lift through there, you're going to lose a lot of time. It's a big compromise all the way around that racetrack."

Development in the nineties has been tough. With Lola cars of Great Britain dominating the fields, only a few others have been successful. Penske's chassis have had good luck, but others have met with dis-

Springs are fitted over the shocks. The threads on the top of the damper can be adjusted effectively lengthening or shortening the pushrod to lower or raise the ride height of the car. One-sixth of a turn of that nut can make a big difference in ride height.

The anti-roll bar can be adjusted by twisting a control device beneath the bodywork. A U-shaped link abates the pushrod—as well as the wheel attached to the other end—from moving any great distance. At the end of the link—at the bottom of the U is what looks like a set of short thin bicycle forks, with a solid bar joining them together just below the driver's feet. The forks control the anti-roll bar. The blades of the two-pronged fork can be turned and tuned. On an oval, the teams would turn the thin side in, creating stiff resistance, making it necessary for the bar to twist. On most road courses they would swivel them so the pliable sides are facing the shocks—in other words, giving the roll bar some slack. Such quick-adjust suspensions are not peculiar to Indy Car racing. NASCAR stock cars, for instance, have long used screw jack set-ups that permit crews to tighten down or loosen the suspension at each corner of the car.

Jimmy Vasser's Lola seems a little unsettled, and is perhaps pushing a bit. The team might change the angles of the upper and lower wishbones legs. The rear of the car will refrain from squatting when the power is applied. One leg—the front leg—will be higher than the rear leg of the upper and lower wishbone. That will help keep the car from squatting under power, which will then make the front end stick more effectively.

astrous results—notably Galles chassis and the Truesports chassis, which was bought and further developed by Bobby Rahal in 1993. Although Lola buyers are free to change the design of the suspension, doing so is at the risk of making the package go backward. Gains can be made only when the playing field is level; that is, only when the suspension being developed is as fast and as competent as the existing designs. Teams find the parity hard to accomplish, let alone exceed. Under this climate, advances in suspension come slowly.

Chapter 9

Power to Burn: The Fuel

Since the beginning of racing, engineers had tried to create a high-compression internal combustion engine. Engineers had always known that higher compression helps burn the fuel and makes the motor more efficient. Simply put, it gives the car more power.

But fuel in the early days was poorly refined stuff. Although there was no octane rating in 1920, the fuel being used—straight pump fuel—would probably have been rated around 50 octane. Compression ratios of more than 4.5:1 or 5:1 caused incessant detonation (pinging) and knocking.

As fuel additives were developed, fuel became a factor that helped advance the Indy Car engine. Benzol was the first racing fuel additive, and was used to reduce detonation, or "pinging." The engine's compression ratios increased, and the engine's performance also improved in direct proportion to the advances. Other fuels which have been studied and used in racing include alcohol, which, with its very high latent heat evaporation, cooled the engine very effectively. And while all fuels will eventually vaporize as temperatures increase, and may detonate prior to ignition, methanol, another form of alcohol fuel, has a lower volatility for detonation.

Through experiments with alcohol additives in the late twenties, race teams found that alcohol practically eliminated overheating problems yet at the same time, the fuel was still resistant to detonation, which had been the bane of performance. In fact, compared to leaded fuel of the day, alcohol could be given an equivalent octane rating. (Alcohol does not have an octane rating on the same scale as gasoline.) Experiments centered on two types of alcohol: grain alcohol and wood alcohol. The ethyl alcohol (grain alcohol) was less efficient, so the methyl alcohol (wood alcohol) was used. The same essential fuel is still used today in Indy Car racing; we call it methanol.

The problem posed by methanol—a problem not found with gasoline—was with consumption. In 1930, with rule changes effectively banning four-stroke, supercharged engines, methanol disappeared. Leaded gasoline gave nearly three times better mileage and carried better octane ratings by that time, allowing engineers to raise the compression ratios to 12:1.

The filler hose is an aircraft style coupling that shuts off as it is unhooked after the refilling has been completed. "Years ago the valves on the pit tanks weren't spring loaded," says Jim Reynolds of Valvoline. "When you opened the valve back then, they were open. That left you [with] a hot fuel tank. If something happened to the hose, it was left open 3in. At Michigan they snapped a hose off. They didn't even get to it. It just gurgled out all 210gal of methanol there on the ground. The valve was left open and somehow or another the fuel apparatus got ripped completely off the thing. The hose is now constructed so that a valve is at the other end of the hose at the pit tank. So at each refueling, there are three fuel men: one who mans the hose, one who handles the vent, and on who opens the valve at the pit tank."

Not exactly space-age stuff, this filler cap did its job, keeping fuel spillage to a minimum. Unfortunately, it lacked the ability to vent property and kept the dangerous gasses contained inside the tank. When the tank ruptured in the event of an accident it often exploded. Ray Touriel

Looking like a cross between a barbecue grill and a bomb, the fuel tank of a circa-1915 Indy Car. The latter description—a bomb—is a more apt description of the tank which is completely unprotected. Filled with common pump fuel at that time, the distilled fuel would have an octane rating (the rating was not devised then) of about 55—making it very similar to something as tame as ordinary kerosine. Compression ratios above five-to-one produced horrible pinging. Nevertheless, the fuel was still highly flammable and caused many terrible injuries. Current tanks are "bulletproof" composite bags which deform to absorb impacts. Ray Touriel

By the late-forties, with the advent of fuel injection (which increased fuel pressure to about 40psi), a blend of gasoline, alcohol, and benzol was usually used. (The benzol was a mixing agent, since gas and alcohol don't mix well.) But engineers found that with fuel injection, straight alcohol could also be used for more power.

Despite all of its wonderful properties, the horrible mileage alcohol provided made it a poor fuel choice. Gasoline enjoyed a renaissance in popularity in the thirties and forties among race teams due to better fuel economy. But power had increased so much during this same period of fuel experimentation that tires wore out more quickly during racing. Tire stops became the reason for pitting—and they also provided plenty of opportunity for refueling. Gasoline lost its appeal since stops for replacement tires were obligatory anyway, and by 1953, everyone ran straight meth-anol. They still do.

Rating Methanol

How is today's fuel rated? If you were to draw a chain of carbon molecules and mix it with hydrogen, the result would be what is called an octane chain. So, using totally unrelated substances as an example, if one molecule of oxygen and two molecules of hydrogen produce water, changing that equation would produce another substance. The same is true for the octane scale. This chain of carbon and hydrogen called octane gives a rating for energy. Hydrocarbons, which are the significant ingredients of the octane rating, are simply a natural way for nature to store energy. The higher the octane rating, the better the energy source. For reference, higher on the scale are propane, butane, heptane, hexane, and octane. The "ane" in octane is actually the energy.

So the petroleum fuel that we call gasoline is nothing more than a carrier of sorts. It holds the hydrocarbons that produce the power that makes our street car move toward the grocery store. Methanol, then is nothing more than a carrier that produces a different sort of energy. Methanol is not on the octane chain, but belongs to an even more complex hydrocarbon chain. But the two fuels can be compared stoichiometrically (stoichiometric is the formula for oxidizing—or completely burning—the fuel. If gas is compressed and ignited, there must be a workable ratio of fuel-to-air to burn the gas completely)

Every pound of gasoline produces 19,000Btus (British thermal units). Methanol burns more quickly and produces around 9800Btus per pound, 52 percent less than gasoline. But methanol will develop 17 percent more power because more of the methanol fuel can be burned with same amount of air. An Indy Car engine will process far more fuel, requiring less air to do it. Fuel is stored in a tank and its delivery is precisely metered. Air, on the other hand, is not so easy to store and deliver.

Gas burns at about 12.6 to 1 (12.6 parts air to 1 part fuel); methanol burns at 6 to 1. Volumetrically, it is possible for a stable road engine to rev high without much detonation. The purer the fuel, the easier the engine is to tune. In fact, gasoline is one of the best energy-producing fuels but is problematic when revved to the quick-breathing rpm of 12,800.

As an example, nitromethane, as used in a Top Fuel dragster, burns at about 1.5 to 1 (1.5 parts air to 1 part fuel required to burn). It produces tremendous power because it needs so little air to ignite. (it is not flammable, however, and will not burn if you try to light it with a match.)

Fueling at an Indy Car Race

Today's fuel comes from one manufacturer—now Valvoline—via the CART board. It can be purchased directly from CART or from the Valvoline-sponsored contingency fund when the driver puts a sticker on the side of the car, which, depending on

Fuel is delivered to the engine from the tank. There is an explicit set of instructions regarding fueling and the amount of fuel that can be used on a given weekend. The reasons for the regulations are mostly for safety. The clear-burning fuel may not be as explosive as gasoline, but it is just as flammable.

The gravity feed tank. Its height and size are limited by Indy-Car and USAC. On Sunday morning (race day), the pit tank will be drained and IndyCar subtracts the amount of the fuel in the car's tank from the amount that's supposed to be in car's fuel tank. The amount is equal to the distance of the race multiplied by 1.8. In other words, the fuel allotment is based on 1.8 miles per gallon—exactly 1.8 gallons.

the level of sponsorship by the oil company, can make the fuel cheaper.

For today's Indy Car racers, there are explicit instructions regarding fueling and the amount of fuel that can be used on a given weekend. The reasons for these guidelines are mostly for safety. The clear-burning fuel may not be as explosive as gasoline, but it is just as flammable.

Valvoline sets up the pumps on Thursday. The teams defuel their cars and go through tech inspection, where safety seals will be put on their tanks. Tanks must hold 40gal of fuel. The CART tech inspector measures each tank to make sure there is no padding inside. Each driver will use about 135-140gal on Friday for practice and preliminary qualifying, and they will draw it from the pit tank. Jim Reynolds, Valvoline's longtime representative, refills the pit tank for Saturday and the team will use approximately the same amount on that second day of qualifying and practice.

On Sunday morning, CART subtracts the amount of the fuel in the car's tank from the amount that's supposed to be there. To determine how much is supposed to be there, the distance of the race is multiplied by 1.8. In other words, the fuel allotment is based on 1.8mpg. *Exactly* 1.8 gallons.

A pit official stands in each pit during the race to monitor the refueling procedures, as well as to ensure that no more fuel is added to the pit tank. If the TV feed is delayed or there is a failed start, the fuel supply will be increased during the race. Valvoline's tanker will drive among the parked Indy Cars and refuel them, based on the loss of the allotted fuel from the time it was allocated to the time the drivers get the command to start their engines. That will be fewer than 3-4gal.

If everything runs like clockwork during the race, there will be no mishaps. If there is a pit road fire, buckets filled with water on the other side of the pit wall are used to extinguish it. Unlike gasoline, methanol is water-soluble. After the race, Valvoline will re-drain the pit tank, put it back in the fueler and bring it back to Ashland Chemical.

Keeping Track of Consumption

The on-board fuel is scrutinized not as it is being used during a race, but prior to the weekend—in fact, prior to the season. CART and USAC mandate a special fuel cell for the storage of fuel in an Indy Car. Made by Goodyear, the cell is a puncture-resistant piece of material over a ballistics-type bag. The rubber is rigid and thick enough that it will stand on its own outside the car. Inside the cell, there are four compartments. Goodyear will construct the cell to the design of the individual make of car (Lola, Penske, or whatever). It sits right behind the driver's back and holds a maximum of 40gal. The team can fill the car from either the right or the left side, depending on the direction the car faces in the pits.

The female parts of the fuel filler system are called "buckeyes"; one will be fitted to the appropriate side of the car before race weekend. The buckeyes hold the sides of the tank and keep it from sloshing. The top of the tank is held up in three places where the vent stack and overflow are.

According to Gary Armentrout of Galles Racing, fuel cells are set up to suit the track configuration at particular events. "If it's an oval track, cars are only turning left and all the fuel runs to the right side of the fuel tank and never rushes back to the left. You have different compartments in your fuel cell, and it has trap doors which allow the fuel to flow [in] one direction but not back the other. When you are on an oval, you turn the doors so that they always make the fuel go to the right so when it gets into the right cell, it doesn't come back to the left. You put your fuel pickup in the right-hand cell. They [the doors] actually swing like little flapper doors, and there is a curtain that divides your fuel cell into several compartments. On each side of that curtain there are two-way doors. Whichever direction you want the fuel to flow, you tie the opposite side door up. There is a little hook in there, and you put a safety tie in there, and the other

This jungle of people on the track surround the cars making up the starting grid. Up in the far left corner the Valvoline truck finishes topping off the cars as they ready for the start. Today's Indy Car fuel comes from one manufacturer via the Indy-

Car board. The fuel can either be purchased directly from IndyCar, or from Valvoline (the current fuel supplier), which sponsors a contingency fund when a race car bears a Valvoline sticker on its side.

110

Topping off with the filler hose prior to the start of the race. Some 7,500gal of fuel are allotted for the field at each Indy Car event, except the Michigan 500, where they will use 15,000gal, and the Indy 500, where they will use 38,000-40,000gal through the month of May. Valvoline invoices Indy-Car $1,250 per car—that's about a dollar a gallon—in an average 300-mile race, IndyCar then bills the teams.

door lets the fuel flow through, but then it closes behind it. So if it wants to slosh back the other way, it can't. The pickups are in the back middle for [a] road course."

The teams want to make sure they get the fuel efficiently delivered up to the top of the engine, with no fuel left at the bottom of the tank. At 1.8mpg, that equals less than 1gal per lap at most tracks on the sixteen-race championship trail. Fuel is precious.

What can be done to improve fuel economy? "Two things are done to help fuel mileage when you don't know if you can finish the race with the fuel you've got," Armentrout says, "One is to short shift; the other is to lean the mixture out. Short shifting means that rather than running to a red-line of, say, 13,000rpm, you'll reduce the rev limits where you shift. You'll back it down 700 or 1000rpm.

"Reducing the fuel mixture is the second thing you'll do to improve fuel economy. They [drivers] adjust the mixture from the cockpit. Optimally, for performance and reliability, you want to run a rich mixture. But if you're not getting mileage, you'll back it down and use a leaner mixture. It increases your mileage and lowers your power. It also makes the engine run a little bit warmer. Methanol keeps it pretty cool. It's way better fuel as far as cooling the engine than gasoline."

Engine cooling has always been determined more by water and oil temperatures than by fuel. Methanol simply helps whatever situation already exists. If the teams converted to gasoline, they might have to increase the size of the cooling system.

Safety is a main concern when considering fuel. CART officials constantly study the refueling process to try to make it even safer. For example, Reynolds says, "Years ago, the valves [on the pit tanks] weren't spring-loaded. When you opened the valve back then, they were open. That left you a hot fuel tank. If something happened to the hose, it was left open 3in. At Michigan, they snapped a hose off. They didn't even get to it. It just gurgled out all 210gal of methanol there on the ground. The valve was left open, and somehow or another, the fuel apparatus got ripped completely off.

"The hose is now constructed so that a valve is at the other end of the hose at the pit tank. So at each refueling, there are three fuel men: one who mans the hose, one who handles the vent, and one who opens the valve at the pit tank."

Chapter 10

Through the Gears: The Transmissions

Power is moderated through the transmission or gearbox. On an Indy Car, the transmission is mounted directly to the back of the motor—bolted on and assimilated into the whole structure of the chassis, like the engine, and becoming a stressed member of the entire package. Compared to that of, say, a Porsche 928, the design of the Indy Car is easy to understand. Where the Porsche has a drive shaft leading from the back of the engine and flywheel back to a rear transaxle, the Indy Car simply eliminates the drive shaft and bolts the engine straight to the bell housing. The engine is behind the driver so the package can be mated directly.

Most gearboxes use a basic H-pattern. Lola cars, run by most teams in 1993 were designed to take a standard gearbox—with the layout as described above. Penske chassis were developed with a transverse box, using a sequential shifter, like a motorcycle shifter. To go through the gears, the driver pushes the shifter forward.

On the 1993 Lola chassis cars, power comes to the back of the transmission via a shaft at the end of which is permanently mounted a first and second gear. Above it, the change gears run on a parallel shaft. Power is put out through a lay shaft, which essentially continues the torque along the same line as the crankshaft. Then it gets more complicated. In a standard front-engine, rear-drive car, such as the 928, the shaft is powered back toward the rear of the transmission and eventually out to the wheels. By contrast, in an Indy Car, the power comes forward. In other words, the transaxle or differential is forward of the change gears. As the driver selects the gears—from one to six—the change gears are moved back and forth on the pinion shaft straight to the ring and pinion. Those gears—above the lay shaft—are the focus of the transmission man.

There are at least four or five combinations of lay shafts. The standard lay shaft is called a fourteen-sixteen. First gear is fourteen teeth and the second gear is sixteen teeth. With the fourteen-tooth gear, the dri-

ver can choose several different mated change gears—usually a forty, forty-one, and forty-two tooth gear. Each set creates a different ratio. The change gears are selected and slide onto the assembly with spacers and a castellated dog ring. Named after the gun turrets in a castle, the rings have cut-out areas that help line up the gears as they are being engaged.

Unlike synchronizing, where the gears actually have a crude clutch that mates a street car's transmission to the next higher or lower gear to be able to shift at any speed and any rev range, the Indy Car

The 1928 Miller Special, driven by Leon Duray. This is the car that Duray put on the pole for the 1928 Indianapolis 500. This was the most successful front wheel drive race car produced at that time. The transverse mounted transmission fits between the seventeen inch space between the frame rail, producing weight for traction on the front end, without the bulk of having the motor placed in the same direction. It was actually a fairly fragile engine due to the thickness of the gears, yet it had a great deal of success. Ray Touriel

transmission's castellated rings are very, very coarse, like something you would find in a tractor. In fact, both transmissions hold very basic components. In order to shift gears (depending on the gear), the driver of a tractor, dump truck, or semi-truck would have to either stop the vehicle or match the revs. The same is true with an Indy Car, but because the gears are matched so well—because the drop-in revs are so small—the driver can just throw it into gear. It will still go in. When somebody misses a shift, it's because he has let his revs drop too much or he has tried to shift too quickly. The "castles" line up the gears in which they are tapered so that when they go in, they pull the dog rings together and keep them together. The castellated rings help the driver select gears quicker and keep the gears from slipping out.

The Transmission Man

The gears themselves are always the focus of the transmission man. At any given racetrack, the crew tries to determine the appropriate set of gears to use on that change gear pinion shaft. Tailoring gears to

the track is a tough job. They concentrate on the best gearing for the track with an eye on "the split," the difference in gears and the corresponding difference in engine revs. The transmission tuner doesn't want his driver to ever be out of the power band. At a race-track like Elkhart Lake, for example, drivers have to deal with a very long straight-aways as well as some very short corners.

Indy teams would concentrate on selecting a fifth gear that would give their drivers about a 150-200rpm drop from the top gear so that he can rev a little higher going through traffic. The cars pull a lot better at a higher rpm, but the engine's longevity isn't as good at the higher revs, and fuel mileage plummets. Second, third, and fourth gears are just for pulling out of the pits and for yellow flag situations. Bad splits can make shifting difficult, but the primary focus will be on the fifth and sixth gears.

To accommodate long corners or straights on a road circuit, teams need a long gear, or short ratio, so they don't over-rev the engine. In that instance, there might be a longer rev drop between gears or more

This car, like many of its time, led different lives and was raced under many different circumstances. Originally, it was a 1935 Miller-Ford front -wheel-drive. Sold to private parties after the 1935 steering linkage failures, It raced again in 1941, the car

was fitted with a Novi V8, finishing fourth. Although it is unknown what the actual history is of this car, the car as it is seen here seems to still have an identity crisis; the grill appears to be off something other than a 1935 Ford. Ray Touriel

113

The Transfer of Power

Nicolas Cugnot is credited with having invented the first self-propelled vehicle. He did so with fairly complicated means of getting the power to the ground: via front-wheel-drive.

As the automobile evolved, most major manufacturers experimented with and ultimately abandoned front-drive cars as being both brutally difficult to handle and poorly suspended. There had always been a natural problem in springing a driven front end while expecting it to steer. The advantage of a front-drive car—then and now—is the huge weight bias over the driven wheels, which enhances traction.

The stories of Barney Oldfield barnstorming the dirt tracks of America in a front-wheel-drive race car epitomize the lore of the early days of racing. Oldfield was a Hulk Hogan of a character; strong and reckless. His cars were fast and powerful—and also difficult to drive. But even in the very early days of racing, front drivers continually showed a superiority to rear-drive cars.

Enter Harry Miller, who began work on a front-wheel-drive car for his driver, Jimmy Murphy, in 1922. Miller's initial designs had the engine mounted in the classic design; that is to say, longitudinally. Murphy had vetoed the transverse engine mounting, citing the resulting horrible handling characteristics. But the longitudinally mounted engine/gearbox setup placed the engine so far back in the frame that the desired gains in traction were almost negated. Traction be damned, Murphy felt; if he was going to try to muscle the car around the track for five hours, he wanted his traction with some degree of controllability.

There were really only two ways of achieving front-wheel drive until Murphy forced a rethink: the transmission was mounted at the end of the crank and flywheel—and sat ahead of the engine to accommodate the front-drive configuration—or it was bolted to the right side of the engine and the output shaft shared a common axis to the crank.

What Miller and his chief engineer Leo Goossen developed was a longitudinally mounted engine with a transversely mounted transmission. In this way, the 17in between the frame was filled, yet the engine was not forced to the rear of the frame.

The power was passed along via a multiple-disc clutch and through a very sophisticated series of telescoping splines to each end of the unit, thereby driving both front wheels. It had a reverse gear and three forward speeds. Although Miller loathed patents, he saw the wisdom in keeping this jewel to himself, and he applied for a patent on the gearbox in 1925.

In addition to the increase in traction, the front-drive cars had a few other advantages: first, with the loss of the huge driveshaft, the cars weighed some 200lb less than their rear-drive counterparts. With the driveshaft absent, the driver could sit lower, reducing the center of gravity and permitting lower bodywork since the driver wasn't sitting up above a driveshaft.

Because of the compact space between the frame, the gears had to be thinner, making the transmission very fragile. Drivers refused to shift gears, preferring instead to have the car push started and keeping it in high gear the entire time. Downshifting was out of the question. Miller had designed what became a very successful component—but not at the hands of Murphy, who was killed at a dirt track race in New York. Nevertheless, by the mid-twenties, most everyone in the Indy Car field had gone to front drivers.

If Miller's front driver was one of his most successful innovations in racing, all-wheel-drive was one of his worst. Financed by the Gulf Oil company, Miller developed a series of cars that, at least on paper, were very competitive. Yet they had been handicapped by the prohibitive weight of an all-wheel-drive design as well as a special pump fuel that Miller was compelled to run per his agreement with Gulf Oil. Given time, perhaps the cars could have been developed, but a garage fire at the Speedway in the early forties claimed all but one of Miller's cars. Miller did not replace the cars.

With the advent of the European Grand Prix cars coming to Indiana in the late thirties, the cars reverted to the traditional front-engine, rear-drive, and they evolved in the United States to what became the classic roadster.

But the prospect of a better way to put the power to the wheels lingered. Novi had been running front-drivers with massive 600lb engines. Traction was one thing, but the Novis could not keep tires on the front as the power and weight of the big powerplant ate tires at twice the speed of the other cars in the field.

The system worked via a set of offset spur reduction gears that were connected to the clutch. The driveline was run down the left side of the car. A limited slip differential split power from front to rear. Again, the system was prohibitively heavy, and the Novis struggled and wore tires badly. Mated to the lighter gas turbine engine of the late sixties, however, the system shined. Unfortunately, it died along with the turbines, which were restricted in 1969.

Front drive has not been around since the emergence of modern era's rear-engine, rear-drive cars. But a few people expect to see a retrospective of sorts eventually (see Jim Hall's comments on aerodynamics in chapter 1). Then as now, front drive provides traction and handling characteristics that all but completely eliminate many inherent flaws of today's Indy Cars. Who knows, Miller's ideas could make a renaissance.

Leon Duray set the world closed course speed record in this front-wheel-drive Miller 91. The record, set at the concrete Packard Proving Ground, stood for twenty four years, illustrating how sophisticated the so-called Golden Age's racing cars really were. Ray Touriel

use of the first or second gears. Teams usually don't use first gear, except for coming out of the pits. Second is not used quite as much as third, which is usually relied upon a great deal. At Elkhart Lake, for example, drivers might use second gear very heavily. There are several corners where the driver will prepare for a long straight that follows, or will hold second through a series of tight corners. At the same time, Elkhart Lake has a Carrousel-type corner, and drivers avoid shifting as they go through it because it upsets the car and unloads the power. They need a car that can hold fifth gear through the corner. They might compromise and use a longer gear while in the corner.

Alex Hering has been responsible for the gearboxes of the Hall VDS Lola for several years, and worked with Teo Fabi on the Porsche transmission as well. Hering has a rare insight into what happens in the Pennzoil Chevy Lola. His input is important to Fabi and the performance of the VDS team. He is both the theory and the application man.

"I can change gears in this gearbox in probably 30 minutes," Hering says. "The way to get to them is that you have a two-sectional back piece. We have

what we call the 'bum,' which is straight through the back, under the wing. So you'd have to remove the wing, remove the one section beneath that, the 'bum,' and there are twelve nuts, and then you have to remove the selector finger by detaching it from the rod.

"The center piece is what contains the shifting forks and everything. It is the master of the change gear parts. So once you undo the tail, you just undo one major nut, and you can slide the whole gear stack off the back of the car with the forks and everything attached.

"The lay shaft is a splined piece, and two gears—first and second gear—are built onto it. Third gear and all the rest of the gears just slide on with spacers to separate them. I have a little stand I set it in and I just work on it there."

The transmission case is left on the end of the engine section. It is never unbolted. For fear of overtorquing or undertorquing the unit, it is separated only occasionally. The gearbox is torqued up to 220lb with Loctite. If the car is warm, having just come in off the track, the mechanics can undo it without using a torch. But if the car has been sitting and is cold, they have to use a small propane torch and a long breaker bar. They work on it with the transmission on the car and the wheels on the ground; the car doesn't have to be in the air. When the gearbox is torqued onto the end of the engine, it is rarely unbolted.

So once the transmission is disassembled, how does the team know which gears to use?

"We'll look at that on the computer and plot the gears by the rev drop," Hering says. "We can tell with the computer what we want the rev drop to be, and it'll tell us what gears to use. So we start from there. At home, before we go, the computer knows what ratios we have, what are available, and where we want to go. Goodyear has a great computer program that they use where you inlay the racetrack into the computer, and it selects what gears you might use by your rpm.

"We have to go to the driver for feel even though the computer starts us out differently. A lot of time, the computer is telling us information from the year before. Things change. The track can be cleaner, dirtier, smoother. The cars have better traction, etc. It's a

problem for the gearbox guy because the traction is starting to take a toll on the gearbox stuff. Now you're able to put more load through the gears.

"At Vancouver, for example, we started out there with certain gears based on the computer, and what we had [was] what we had there [in 1992] with John [Andretti]. We have a 30mph corner, but we have a straight-away that has a top speed of 160mph. So he'd [the crew chief would] look at that, and we'd say 'OK, for sixth gear, I'm going to use a 25-30 which, at the end of the straight, would hopefully give us 12,800 or 13,000rpm. It's got a 35mph corner, so we don't want the power band to go less than 10,500 or 11,000rpm because we only want to see a 2500rpm drop or so.

"Friday morning, we went 90 miles. By the next session, an hour later, we changed second gear, third gear; we left fourth, we changed fifth, and we changed sixth. All of the changes were shorter. But for some reason, we left fourth. So at some spot for him [Teo Fabi], it was perfect. For Saturday morning, he wanted a different second gear all of a sudden. We didn't go short enough apparently, and he wanted to

The front-wheel-drive cars of the twenties were far more clumsy than these Fords of 1935. Harry Miller, who led the design team which brought the ten Fords to Indy, made inroads into both the suspension as well as the aerodynamics of the components. As always, Miller's cars were impeccably prepared. Ray Touriel

go shorter yet. For qualifying, he wanted to make fifth gear shorter, too. We kept sixth because we were already peaked out on the straight-away. For the race, we changed to a different ratio in fourth, fifth, and sixth—we went longer for better mileage."

It's Always Changing

And it all changes again. Before each race, the team will change each and every gear—not for ratios, but for dependability. The team doesn't want a worn gear to shorten race day and take them out of competition, so they replace each gear with a fresh new one.

A general rule of thumb is that if a gear has mileage on it, it should be replaced; 700-1,000 miles is about all a team would want to run on one gear. Even if it looks sound, a gear with this kind of mileage should be replaced.

Classic problems related to gearboxes come when the stress on the gears cause them to split. The split usually manifests itself immediately as a broken tooth on the gear. Teeth also get chipped off when the driver has worn the castellation and forces it into the gear. Regardless of how it happens, a driver with a tooth floating around in the case will know when he's about to have a transmission problem. It will run very rough. He'll feel something wrong with it right away, as the bits floating around in the transmission attack and work their way between everything else, forcing the shafts apart and breaking them.

Rough pavement or changes in pavement surfaces causes the tires to bounce and leave the ground. Ideally, those kinds of forces are taken up by the shafts. The drive shaft and input shafts are designed to have enough length to take windup for that reason. It just twists up and relieves itself afterwards. On a street circuit, however, loads are higher. They don't necessarily all get taken up. And the amount of time drivers spend shifting on bumpy surfaces hurts the gearbox. Some guys will get in and off the power several times through a bumpy corner. Regardless of how the drivers apply power, the shafts are constantly winding up and letting go. Try it in your own car. If you get on and off the throttle, you're creating the same condition—except Indy Car drivers are trying to get the rear tires loose so that they can swing the rear end through the corner because, perhaps, they're trying to drive around an understeering problem and they're doing it with probably four times more horsepower than you have.

The life of a transmission can be extended by a gentle foot on the throttle. Drivers who watch the bumps and drive through with an even throttle can keep the gearbox stresses to a minimum. At the same time, the clutch is there—although not all drivers use it.

"It depends on the driver," Hering says. "Like our driver, Teo, he uses the clutch all the time. He uses it for upshifts and downshifts. There are some drivers

Transmissions—especially in the front-wheel-drive cars—were often temperamental components that drivers tried their best to avoid using. Whether two speeds or five, the more time shifting gears meant the more chances to destroy something. Ray Touriel

who don't use the clutch—like Rahal. I believe he doesn't use the clutch very often."

To Shift or Not to Shift

For some, whether to shift with or without the clutch is a critical decision. Rumor had it that at Bettenhausen Racing, which used a Penske chassis and a transverse gearbox in 1993, driver Stefan Johansson was told not to use the clutch, that he couldn't use the clutch pedal at all, other than when leaving the pits.

The transverse gearbox contains a beveled gear. Instead of the shifting gears being in line with the crankshaft, they're turned sideways by means of this beveled gear. Then the shifting gears are sideways in the box on the same axis of the axles or the drive shafts. The transverse layout was developed most successfully by Roger Penske to tighten up the package. In other words, putting the gearbox on the traditional Lola-style transmission makes the package longer. But turning the gears sideways produces a very tight "butt" and shorter tail. The

Seen from behind, an Indy Car's transmission appears to be metallic and workmanlike, a contrast to the suspension components and the engine, which are covered by smooth body- *work. Note at the very base of the transmission housing is a splined coupling for the external starters that fire up Indy Car engines.*

wheelbase is the same, but aerodynamic drag was improved.

"Penske and Truesports are now the only teams using transverse gearboxes with the gears at right angles to the center line of the car, whereas the Hewland runs longitudinal," said famed long-time Truesports team boss Steve Horne. "And we did this for aerodynamic reasons because if the gears are at right angles to the center line of the car, you can cram a lot more into a shorter space and you can gain some aerodynamic advantage of the car. It was also [a] function of the aerodynamics, basically. Eighty percent of the reasoning was because it was a function of the aerodynamics."

But since most teams don't have the luxury—or, perhaps, the pain—of having their own chassis, they simply get what comes with the car. As the 1994 season loomed, the switch to transverse gearboxes looked to be the wave of the future, with Lola and Reynard joining the ranks of those using the new layout.

"Most of our cars are built by Lola," explained Al Unser, Jr,. before his switch to Penske in 1994, "and

as soon as Lola makes transverse transmissions, then I think you'll see a lot of other teams having that. But right now, it's exclusive to Penske, because he builds his own rear ends. And it is very, very costly to be building your transmission from scratch."

Of course, the transmission has to be mated to the engine somehow. As in any street car with a manual transmission, that coupler is a clutch. Although allowed in Formula One cars, automatic or semi-automatic transmissions are not allowed in Indy Car racing, so the clutch is still used and the driver still has to change gears manually.

Mounted directly on the flywheel like all standard clutches, the common unit is a three-plate dry clutch with three friction plates sandwiched together. Made of sintured metal—essentially a textured and abrasive alloy—the clutch is typically spring-plated with diaphragmed spring plates. Some teams previously used carbon fiber pads, but they have been banned.

Either way, the clutch has a tough job. Fairly small when compared to a street car's clutch, the unit is only about 6in across. Racers don't want the big flywheel desired in street cars because they don't need the smoothness it provides. Just the opposite is true: The flywheel needs to be small to keep kinetic energy low and to allow the crankshaft to remain positioned almost on the ground for the best possible center of gravity. Plus, there's the "packaging" to consider. The tunnels under the car make it impossible to increase the diameter of the clutch assembly. The only way to make things work is to make the package small.

Because of its size, the clutch assembly continues getting more fragile. Materials are thinner to make the weight lighter, which compromises the reliability of the clutch. An increased load is accommodated through a smaller-diameter unit, when what is really needed is a bigger diameter that takes less force to clamp. It's just like a disc brake. If you could use bigger discs on the wheels, you could get more performance with less heat and less stress.

That having been said, teams don't have clutch problems during a race, as a rule. If anything, they have throw-out bearing problems because the bearing they use is small. They could use a larger unit, but don't because of weight. Like so many other components of a race car, throw-out bearings are reliable for only 500 miles.

Not only is the rear wing mounted to the transmission, it is also a major area for mounting the suspension as well.

Problems related to gearboxes come when the stress on the gears cause them to split. The split usually manifests itself immediately as a broken tooth on the gear. A driver with a tooth floating around in the case will know when he's about to have a transmission problem. The bits floating around will just attack everything and eventually the bits will start getting in between everything else, forcing the shafts apart and breaking them. In addition, rough pavement or changes in pavement surfaces causes the tires to bounce and leave the ground. Those kinds of forces are (the designers and crew hope) taken up by the shafts. The drive shaft and input shafts are designed to have enough length to take windup for that reason. It just twists up and relieves itself afterwards.

Chapter 11

Traction on the Track: The Tires

Indy Car tire development has occurred over the years at one of two speeds: frantic breakneck pace or slug-like progression.

And tires have probably contributed to the overall safety and performance of the sport far more than any other single component. Tire wars—competition among tire suppliers—have moved the technology along with surprising alacrity, and during the periods when there was only one tire maker for Indy Cars, the focus inevitably turned to safety.

Indy Car tires of the teens and early 20s used fabric carcasses on clincher rims. The fabric developed a great deal of heat as the tires rolled, usually doubling the pressure from 50 to 100lb in just a few laps. They were clamped onto wooden spoke wheels and could be removed in about 1min. The average car used just two sets in the 500 miles.

European manufacturers first brought wire wheels and slip-off hubs to the Indy Car field in 1913, followed in 1915 by the first cord tire with knock-off hub nuts. When struck with a mallet, these hubs would spin all the way off the threads and fall to the ground. Pit stop speed improved dramatically. At the same time, manufacturers discovered that reducing the amount of fabric in the tire kept it from heating up so fast, and pit stops were reduced.

Until the twenties, tire manufacturers didn't really make tires for Indy. The balloon tire from Firestone—dubbed the Speedway Special—was the first purpose-built racing tire. The balloon was not only wider, which put more rubber on the ground than the traditional straight-sided cord tire, but it also could be underinflated—at 30lb—to achieve maximum bite on the track. Speeds were up 25mph in 1925. Firestone pretty much monopolized the sport for the next several decades, and didn't do much development after the balloon. But in 1953, tires started on a journey that has only recently ended with the Goodyear radial.

The first big change occurred in 1953, when tread was increased by 1.5in. Wheels began to grow larger again, sometimes reaching 20in, giving them a bigger footprint. Compounds had developed to a point where they stuck the car to the ground much better, and more rubber meant that they wore well. In fact, the wear was so good that a driver could run a complete race on a single set of tires.

In 1963, Firestone developed a smaller tire for a 15in Halibrand wheel. The drop from 18in to 15in caused some alarm that the footprint wouldn't be large enough, so Firestone increased the width another 1.5in. Lap speeds immediately jumped, and teams scrambled for both wheels and tires.

That seemed as good an opportunity to enter racing as any, and the Goodyear Tire and Rubber Company began offering its racing tires in 1963, ultimately creating the contemporary prototype for race tire wars. As Leo Mehl, Goodyear's director of racing, explains, it was a decision prompted by a need that wasn't being addressed by Firestone.

"What they did was they were running little, narrow tires, and nobody liked them," Mehl says. "[A.J.] Foyt came and got us. Firestone was running those little, skinny tires, and Lotus came with Dunlop on the rear-engined cars, and Foyt asked for the Dunlops on his roadsters. They told him they weren't for roadsters; that they wouldn't last. Foyt said, 'Hey, it's my butt, let me try them.' But they wouldn't do it. That's when he got on a plane, and went to Akron, Ohio, and knocked on the door of the chairman of the board [at Goodyear] and asked if we could help him. That was in 1963. That was over tire performance. [Firestone] pulled it out after that. [The Goodyear tires] had the ability and they had the performance. It took us five years to finally beat them. But we were very determined that wouldn't happen to us, so we're constantly trying to update them. We keep working at it because we don't want to do what Firestone did when we came in."

By the end of the 1968 season and taking place in just over a year, tire widths almost doubled; profiles dropped and created fantastic lateral stiffness; tread compound improved; and lap speeds jumped

Mario Andretti leads a Dan Gurney Eagle into a corner in 1966. Andretti would win this race as well as eight others that season, ultimately clinching the Indy Car title. Note the size of the tires, which had increased in width, decreased in profile, and had been enhanced in both adhesion and reliability. Speeds rose quickly with the new tire technology. The Milwaukee Mile/ Russ Lake

10mph. By the end of the sixties, the typical Indy Car tire was 12in across and had a "forty series" profile (the profile was 40 percent as wide from the bead to the top of its outermost diameter as it was tall, when ten years earlier, the typical tire was taller than it was wide), and was far stickier.

Even though Dunlop (whose tires were run on Jimmy Clark's Lotus), was really a road racing tire, it couldn't compete on an Indy Car, so it was essentially a battle between Goodyear and Firestone, a battles which Goodyear ultimately won. Firestone left Indy Car racing in 1975 and Goodyear has been on its own ever since—although perhaps not for long, as in 1993 Firestone announced plans to supply tires for Indy Car racing in 1995.

The Use of Radial Tires

The radial tire, which all Indy Cars now use, was developed by Goodyear in 1984, but first appeared in August 1986. Inconsistency has always been the bane of racing tires, but in 1988, a more consistent stagger was developed and by 1990, the tires were extremely consistent.

"We used to come to a road course and we'd have hundreds of punctures," Mehl says. "One of the biggest factors with going to the radials was to get rid of punctures. Durability on a radial is very tricky. A bias tire is very forgiving. They way you lay the ply in there, if you're off a quarter of a degree or something, maybe you have a stagger problem or something. But in a radial, if you don't put every piece in there absolutely right, it loses air. The requirement for precision in a radial is much higher."

Goodyear now offers four major radial tires for Indy Car racing: the Speedway Eagle, the Superspeedway Eagle, the Road Course Eagle, and the Eagle Rain. Tire costs range from $250 for a front tire to $350 for a rear tire—and Goodyear loses money on

Magnesium wheels appeared on Indy Cars about 1953 and became a fixture by the late fifties. The combination of weight—and the constant goal of reducing unsprung weight—and the absence of having to true wires on a regular basis made the cast wheels a true blessing. Ray Touriel

the deal. The limit for each race car is twenty-eight tires per normal event; forty-four are allowed for the Indy 500 and the 500-mile Michigan race.

The alternative. Wire wheels were difficult to keep adjusted and time consuming as well. The cast magnesium—or even the steel wheels—were far superior in terms of man-hours spent in upkeep. The magnesium wheel equalled the weight of the wire wheel, giving the unit descent strength without the hassles. Designers still hadn't agreed upon the optimum size for a wheel. Some felt it was better to increase the size to keep the footprint larger and thereby increase the wear. Ray Touriel

At Indy, the cars run about 75 miles on a tank of fuel. That means most teams change the outside tires every two stops; the inside front tire gets changed every three stops, and the inside rear tire can usually remain on the car the entire distance of the race but is changed with the front left tire. During a caution period, the entire set will usually be replaced since there is time to do so.

Teams will "scuff" the tires prior to the race itself so that they have built up a heat cycle. The scuffed tires will also be checked for balance and mounting.

Chassis manufacturers usually supply the wheels, so a Lola car will have Lola wheels, and so on. The wheels are typically cast-magnesium, with 10-14in widths, 15in diameters, and a channeled design similar to that of a street car for safety in the event of a tire failure. A safety device locks the wheels onto the hubs after the quick pits stops.

Superspeedway tread width on the front tires is 10in, mounted on a 10in-wide wheel. (Regulations stipulate that front wheels measure a maximum of 15x10in.) The tires weigh 16lb. Superspeedway rear tires are matched differently, or staggered, as will be explained shortly.

Tire inflation is an important part of the equation. Heat changes the pressure in the tires. The optimum shape for ultimate performance of the tire is created in a mold, but is controlled by the pressure inside the tires. The movement of the tires, or deflection, is controlled by the pressure inside the tires. Tires are traditionally underinflated to compensate for the change in pressure as the tire itself and the air inside it heat up. They are filled cold according to how much they are expected to heat up. In other words, if the engineers expect 51lb of pressure during the race, they will fill the tire to, say, 38lb pressure before the race. The formula of pressures changes, depending on such things as the track, the ambient temperature, and the setup. But the normal setup for a Superspeedway Eagle is 38lb per square inch of cold air on the right front, 34lb on the left front, 36lb on the right rear, and 34lb on the left rear. If conditions suggest that the tires will heat only a few degrees under operating conditions, and the team guesses wrong, the tire will perform badly. If the tires are too cold, or if pressure is low, the tires will blister the outside edges. In extreme circumstances, the bead can separate and the tire will deflate. Overinflated tires tend to rise in the middle, causing blistering at best and, at their worst, uncontrollability from a smaller footprint area.

The pressure differences between right and left tires are necessary because of the differences in demands on the right and left sides of the car. For example, on an oval, the car is constantly turning left. The performance of the right tire, therefore, is more critical than that of the left. Because all the weight will transfer to the front as it enters a corner and slows down, the right front tire—will eventually get up to

51psi and will most likely wear the worst. The right rear will also wear a great deal.

The rear tires weigh about 23lb each. The left rear is inflated to 34lb cold and that pressure will increase to 41lb during a race. The right rear is usually inflated to 36lb cold and is expected to reach 48lb during a race. Since the belt on a radial tire makes it difficult to over-inflate or underfill them, racing tires have become much more consistent. Says Mehl, "If a guy gets a good setup in practice, he doesn't lose it with a radial."

Tire Stagger

Unlike the front tires, the rear tires are different sizes from side to side. This difference is called "stagger." It helps the car turn into the corner easier. If the inside (left) tire is smaller than the outside, the car will have a tendency toward the inside of the oval. The diameter of the right tire is set at 27.1in, but that of the inside tire can vary between two stagger sizes: 26.92in or 26.86in. Theoretically, it does the same thing as a differential.

The knockoff spoke wheel of the twenties fitted with an early clincher tire. The wire wheel replaced a wooden spoked wheel that had cotton-carcassed tires bolted onto them. Most cars in the early days of the Indy 500 used about a dozen sets of tires per race. The tires could be changed in about a minute. This time was cut down substantially with the advent of the knock-off hub, which would come spinning off onto the ground with one prodigious blow from a mallet. Ray Touriel

This Firestone tire was made popular during the 1948 season some. Tire designs had changed very little since the thirties, only changing in compound slightly over the years. In 1954 they were widened and nylon cord was used for the first time in the bias ply tires, prolonging the life of the tires. In 1963 Goodyear got involved with racing and the tires changed dramatically. Ray Touriel

As you can see, the differences are very slight in actual dimensions, but the changes can make a huge imbalance in the lap charts. Stagger is referred to by numbers; the number relates to the difference between the two tires. By asking for an "18," the driver is looking for a set that is 18/100in different from side to side.

"You know, we took two staggers to Indianapolis [in 1992]," Mehl says. "You could come to Goodyear and get an 18in stagger or a 25in stagger, and what you're talking here is 7/100ths of an inch difference between the two. [He folds a piece of paper into eight pieces.] The difference of what we're talking about—the difference between making a car push and making a car loose—is this much here.

"One time, Danny Sullivan thought he was going to be on the pole at Indy. He says, 'I wanted a 25in stagger and all I got was a 21in. And the car wouldn't come out.' It's real. Absolutely real. That much difference, honest to goodness, makes the difference between the car being loose or the car pushing."

Sullivan explains the feel. "It was probably a combination of everything. But I remember it changed the car from loose to push, or vice versa. I changed it, and it changed the car. You can feel that. We also know how many laps the tires will last during a race. So what you have to do from a driver's point of view is that you'll see a lot of guys going really fast at the beginning and they might fall off, or you might see some guys going slower at the beginning of the race and [they] save their tires."

Tires have probably contributed to the overall safety and performance of the sport far more than any other single component. Tire wars have moved the technology along with surprising alacrity; and during the periods where only one tire maker produced wares for Indy Cars, the focus inevitably turned to safety.

Drivers who can feel their tires' stage of wear are apt to be quicker, using the optimum performance of the tires to their advantage, but avoiding a slip when the tires begin to deteriorate during the race.

"We know exactly when they're going to go off," Sullivan elaborates concerning the loss of effectiveness and grip. "You could see guys go fast for two laps and then slow right down. Then they'd go fast again. The reason they did that was entirely because of the tires. The tire wasn't really capable of doing three qualifying laps. It lost its performance. Now, it would still be fast, but it would be off a couple of tenths here and there. That's quite a bit.

"You might find a particular circuit where the tire suits your particular style. Some guys are better at feeling what a tire could do at a particular track. Rick Mears was good, particularly good at the superspeedways. He could tell if the tire or the suspension."

If the drivers can feel the tires going away—and Goodyear feels they probably can or should be able to—then the manufacturer has learned to accommodate this driver's that skill in tire development.

"We have gradually improved the road course tire," says Mehl. "We introduced radials in road courses, then introduced radials at short ovals, then we introduced radials at Indy, and finally we introduced radials in Michigan. That was a tough transition, but we've been very conservative with the compounds because we really try to go fast. Conservative means not trying to get lap speeds. What you're trying to get now is a tire that runs forty laps without dropping off the speed. Basically, every race tire starts fast, but

then it starts to get hot, and starts to break down a little bit. It may not be strictly be heat. We haven't found really what it is. It may be [that] the surface gets worn down.

"We have race tires at certain tracks that will drop off [in performance and speed]. At tough tracks like Bristol, you can drop off 5-6mph. At road courses you will drop off a second, two seconds, and now you don't worry about that. I mean, it depends [on whether] this compound, this construction, this tire will run at this speed pretty consistently. The guy gets [that when] the car [is] set up; it doesn't start to get loose or doesn't start pushing. It stays consistent.

"When we had the bias [ply] tires, a half-pound of air would make a difference. So we were absolutely dead before we even started with the bias tires to try to give them the kind of precision they needed at In-

In one season, tire widths almost doubled, the profiles dropped creating fantastic lateral stiffness, tread compound improved, and lap speeds jumped 10mph. By the end of the sixties, the typical Indy Car tire was 12in across and was a forty series profile (the profile was 40 percent as wide from the bead to the top of the tire's outermost diameter as it was tall). Ten years earlier they had been taller than they were wide and far stickier. Pictured here is the latest evolution, the Goodyear road course radial mounted to the now outlawed disc-style wheel.

There are four major radial tires currently available from Goodyear: the Speedway Eagle, the Superspeedway Eagle, the Road Course Eagle, and the Eagle Rain. Tires cost between $250 for a front tire and $350 for a rear—and Goodyear loses money on the deal. For the amount of tire development they do, the price is quite reasonable. Teams are limited to twenty-eight tires per event; forty-four are allowed for the Indy 500 and the Michigan race. Pictured here are a set of Goodyear's Eagle Rains.

dianapolis. You used to watch the three guys who were leading the race come into the pits, and then you'd never see them again. They were just gone. What happened was the teams were keeping fifteen staggers in their pits, and when they went out, if they left the pits differently from the first time, it would change the air pressure, which would change the stagger. Oh, it was terrible. That's what they were always talking about: 'I got a bad set.' They didn't get a bad set of tires; the balance went off.

"It's not like a spark plug, where you can lose consistency in one and still have a car that runs well. Most components won't affect the car as much as a tire. The thing absolutely has to have four tires that are absolutely the same size with the same construction. They are so critical on a high-speed course like Indianapolis."

But what about road courses? Well, remember that regular speedway tires weigh about 15 percent more than road course tires. The staggered tire is about 1/4in smaller than the corresponding right 27.1in tire, to allow for quicker turns on the short ovals. For running on road courses, no stagger is generally used. The front tires are 10in wide, have 25.5in diameters, and weigh about 18lb, while the rears are 14.3in wide, have 27.8in diameters, and weigh 25.5lb.

Road courses have different demands than ovals. Tires are subjected to much more down force than at the ovals. Although the cars are constantly traveling at a good clip at an oval track like Indy, at most road courses, there are several straight-aways where speeds will reach 200mph before a driver must slow to 50mph for a turn shortly afterward.

Advances in tire technology build on empirical data, and while recent changes have been small, electronic technology has made the whole process easier.

"The first thing you do with a tire," Mehl says, "is make it on a computer and do a simulated test. We can simulate Indianapolis or any road course. We've got a pretty good system now. It used to drive us crazy when we'd go to a new circuit and we'd have to figure out what the tires were like. Like when they change three corners at Long Beach every year, what do you think that's going to do? How's it going to affect the tire? Now we just simulate it."

Breaking Loose

When a driver exceeds his tires' limits by either going too fast in a particular corner or due to an abrupt change of direction from an altercation on the track, the result is a spin. The tires break loose from the pavement, and the kinetic energy, which had been controlled through the footprints of the tires, is unleashed. That energy has wanted to keep the car going in a straight line all day. Up until the point of the slide, the inclination toward the straight line has been abated. As soon as the tire breaks off, however, the car goes in that straight line as it's wanted to. The worst possible result is the car hitting the wall and the driver leaving the circuit in an ambulance. On a more minor level, the tires' breaking loose will simply result in flat-spotting the tires, which is much more common in road racing than in oval racing because of the huge aerodynamic differences between a road course car and an oval track car; the down force is quite different.

Danny Sullivan's 1985 Indy 500 win was accomplished after a spectacular spin at full speed. After narrowly missing Mario Andretti, whom he had just passed for the lead, Sullivan pitted, changed tires, and raced back to the checkered flag.

Air pressure is critical, and it will change during operation. Tire engineers must anticipate the increase in pressure ahead of time. Wheels are usually supplied by the chassis manufacturers. The wheels are typically cast magnesium and are 10-14in in width and 15in in diameter, with a channeled design similar to a street car for safety in the event of a tire failure.

Says Sullivan, "When I spun at Indy, it was almost like it was such a quick spin that there were no big wings on it, and when the car's going sideways, you're losing all the down force. That's why cars on superspeedways don't slow down that much before they hit the wall or something. There's no down force on the car, except when it's going forward. If you spin [at a road course], you have a high down force wing with a lot of down force and it really kind of grinds the tire and flat-spots it. It wasn't so much that I was forced to come in [at Indy]; I could have kept going. I slightly flat-spotted the tires, and that brought out a yellow flag because of the spin, so it was as good a time as any to come in and make sure nothing was broken and put new tires on."

So what does a flat-spotted tire feel like from the driver's point of view? "It's like a big vibration," Sullivan says. "It's not uncontrollable usually. But I've flat-spotted them so badly that it is. You can hardly drive the thing. But then you've probably damaged them so badly you can't continue anyway. The problem is, during the race, what are you going to do, stop?"

Formula One cars are much more prone to flat-spotting their tires than Indy Cars, which is why you'll hear the Formula One track announcers using the term so much more. First, the cars weigh about 30 percent less, so they can afford to have a softer tire compound. The softer the compound, the more it acts like a big eraser, quickly wearing away the rubber at the point where it is sliding and scrubbing itself on the pavement. Second, the Formula One car always places a premium on down force and grip. The tires are smaller, and teams are constantly fighting to improve grip. So when it lets loose, there's a great deal more down force pushing the tires in the pavement.

"The Indy Car tire is different from a Formula One tire," says ex-Grand Prix driver-turned Indy Car driver Eddie Cheever. "It has to be. It has to run at places like Indy. And it has to be able to put up with the demands a place like Indy puts on it so the driver doesn't become a speck when he hits the wall."

Hoping for the Best at Indy

Indianapolis brings several problems that are specific to American racing—and to the Speedway at Indy itself. Although the Michigan 500 is a very similar race, it is not as critical as the Indy 500, where everyone strives to do the absolute best. In the showcase that is the Indianapolis 500, drivers, manufacturers, teams, and even tire manufacturers strive to have their product perform its best. Often, a driver's performance is hampered by circumstances beyond his control. Take the 1992 Indy 500 for example.

"I'll tell you," says Mehl with an ironic chuckle, "I've got a history of weather since they've held the Indy 500. We went to the weather bureau after the [1992] race. We said, 'Man, what happened here?'"

The 1992 Indy 500 was one of the most event-filled races run at the Speedway in recent years. A cold spell set upon the Brickyard on Memorial Day weekend, playing havoc with tires. From the parade lap, when Roberto Guerrero crashed before the race even started, to Rick Mears' crash on a late restart, the weather caused slick conditions that the tire engineers were not ready for.

"Cold tires have been a problem ever since I've been in the business," Mehl says. "Who usually experiences cold tires are road racers—endurance racers. But they are all very careful and well-trained to go out and warm the tire up. The harder the tire is, the more you have to warm it up. We ran into a problem that day because two things were happening. First of all, it was the coldest day in the history of the Indianapolis [500]. It was 39deg in the morning and 52deg when the race started. And the lowest it has ever been in the history of the Indy 500 when the race started was 63deg. So it was 10deg colder than it had ever been and in addition to that it had been a very cold night. The cars are so aerodynamic and designed to get so much down force from the wings and bodies [that when they] get the [green] flag at 75 or 80mph, well, they don't have any grip. The grip goes up exponentially. So at 80mph, you have the worst of two worlds: You don't have much grip because the tires haven't warmed up, plus you don't have any down force. Guys who had the car pointed straight were OK; guys who were coming out of the corner—especially turn four—kept ending up in the turn four fence.

"We analyzed that thing. I think there were thirteen crashes. I think about half of them were from cold tires. We got credit for them, all of them, of course," Mehl grinned again, with a resigned look that smelled of fate and bad luck. "The other half were people just bumping into each other.

"You have a situation where you are pretty much obligated to supply one tire for a whole month of weather conditions. Cold at the beginning to maybe an 80deg day on a variety of cars from a 1991 whatever to a 1993 Penske Lola. You have to make one tire to fit every driver, every engine, different horsepowers, good chassis, bad chassis. That's the problem you have with a [tire manufacturing] monopoly. It doesn't make sense that the tire for [the] 1991 Galmer is the same for the 1993 Penske. So what you're required to do is make doggone sure that [it works] at the top end, where the guys are gong really fast."

Tire Wars to Resume

Indy Car racing has been blessed—or cursed, depending on your point of view—by the lack of competition. Firestone's return to the circuit after an absence of nearly two decades brings several new concerns. Although a second manufacturer certainly brings some good things to the table, there are as many disadvantages. "Because it's only Goodyear here at the moment, we have much tougher, stronger tires," Sullivan says. "That will more than

The rubber collects and moves as the tire warms. When it eventually comes off, it rolls into balls that are swept to the outside of the track; drivers call them "marbles," and say that to run up high out of the groove is to run up in the marbles. Teams will "scuff" the tires so they have built up a heat cycle prior to the actual race. The scuffed tires will also have been checked for balance and mounting while they are being scuffed.

likely change when Firestone comes in. I think it will be a little more of a tire war. That's why when they're talking about speed and everything, that's all well and good, but as soon as you have a tire war, all that goes out the window."

Easy-off single-nut hubs make tire changes quick and easy. A safety device that positively locks the wheels onto the hubs after the quick pits stops also exists.

Tire wear is a function of the track, and part of a driver's savvy is his ability to save the tires. In this photo, the wear on the left front tire on Didier Theys' car is obvious.

Clearly, drivers have a concern over the escalating speeds. Consider that while Goodyear put emphasis on safety rather than performance in recent years, Indy Car tires have been fairly stagnant. With the pending tire war, however, tire engineers now have a dilemma: Do they purposely keep the tire slow (and safe), or do they concentrate solely on performance? The latter alternative may be unavoidable in a tire war.

"We have been extremely conservative with the Indy Car tires over the years," Mehl says. "If you got a monopoly, [safety is] really the most important consideration... [With competition from a second tire maker], it will change the strategy significantly. You will go for speed. Speed is not now a consideration. You do want enough grip to keep the driver safe."

"I remember the [tire] wars in Formula One," Eddie Cheever says. "It was a nightmare. Sometimes we'd go through forty sets of tires in a weekend. Goodyear will continue making a tire that is safe and will perform. Goodyear gets a lot of good out of racing. Firestone saw an advantage to racing."

For twenty years, the biggest concern for the Indy Car sanctioning bodies has been to slow the cars down. Everything in racing is about gaining more speed so, obviously, the cars keep getting faster than the tracks on which they run. Goodyear has tried to hold the engineers back so they do not add to that problem. When they introduced the radials, they weren't any faster than the bias tires. They were, however, more consistent and certainly wore a lot better and resisted punctures much better. Safety was being addressed.

"All this stuff sounds wonderful, but the final proof's in the pudding," Mehl says. "The tough part of racing is that you've got to go do it in public. It happens quite regularly, and then you go to a race-track and something changes. Either you'll find that the guys find a new way to set up the cars so they go a second faster, or the track conditions changed, or it got a lot hotter than it ever has before, or whatever. So the problem with tire wars is that sometimes when you're going for speed, your margin isn't as great as it

Up until the tire wars began in the late sixties, speedway tires looked strikingly similar to street tires (under man's hands). In 1968 all that changed as the industry stepped up performance of racing tires (on ground). Traction skyrocketed, speed shot through the roof and it was clear that these were no street tires. Goodyear Tire & Rubber Co.

Danny Sullivan, who produced the world famous "Spin and Win" at the 1985 Indy 500. "When I spun at Indy... I could have kept going. I slightly flat spotted the tires and that brought out a yellow flag because of the spin, so it was as good a time as any to come in and make sure nothing was broken and put new tires on."

was when you had a nice, comfortable monopoly. But then, conversely, the value to you increases a thousand-fold when you actually beat somebody. You learn a lot more with competition. Not only do you learn more, your customer appreciates you more. The publicity you get is a thousand times more. As long as you have a monopoly, the only time you think about tires is when a guy comes flopping down the front straight-away."

What Mehl and Goodyear do not want to repeat was the embarrassing situation that happened in NASCAR's Winston Cup series in the late-eighties. Goodyear had dominated NASCAR tracks for some seventeen seasons, and had relaxed, tempting Hoosier to enter NASCAR in a big way. The David caught Goliath sleeping. Hoosier won several races, and the field of stock cars began to take the small tire

maker seriously enough that Goodyear's reputation was bruised. Goodyear cranked up the heat and eventually outperformed Hoosier again. Had it been a better challenge, the outcome might have been different.

In the final analysis, besides the aerodynamics of the car, tires have a great deal to do with performance. As Mehl says, tires are only the focus when something goes wrong with them. They are expected to work flawlessly, and are only mentioned when they fail. Should the tire wars heat up again, more races may be won or lost as a direct result of the tires.

"Tires, I think, are still a little bit of a black art," Danny Sullivan says. "Because nobody really knows what's going on. With all the technology, with everything they're doing even with computers and things like that, I don't think they can make a perfect tire for a perfect track. Some years they're good at one track, some years they're not."

Usually, they're pretty darn good.

enties. Then, of course, the racing community started waking up a little bit, making changes, reducing the capacity of fuel, ozone, and so forth. Now the technology is such that [the fuel] sits behind the driver, and you don't even know it's there.

"The drivers didn't talk about it because you were supposed to accept that element of danger in a race car. But as time progressed and deaths occurred, you know, a lot of us got a little smarter and started addressing not only race car safety, but track safety. And when it comes to circuit safety, I think Jackie Stewart was quite a crusader in that area. A lot was achieved in Formula One under pressure from drivers' demands. Today, no one is concerned about what anyone would think if you are going to express some opinions. The only thing we think about is how we should improve things we do. That, as a matter of fact, is good about the current environment; they offer encouragement. The sanctioning bodies definitely welcome any input from drivers. And from that, we have achieved a lot."

A huge understatement. Jovy Marcelo died in 1992 at the speedway. But before that, one would have to look back as far as 1982 and the death of Gordon Smiley to find a fatality—at least at Indy.

It seems odd to think about a sport where the losers are calculated in body counts, but racing has sometimes been thought of in that respect. Drivers of the fifties and sixties lost friends as the sport claimed lives on an all-too-regular basis. Racers seemed to be apathetic about their own well-being.

Some of the injuries occurred when there didn't seem to be an alternative. It was a dangerous sport. When a driver hit a wall in a roadster, the car was so stiff and so strong that the damage done to the car was usually minimal. The shock of the impact went

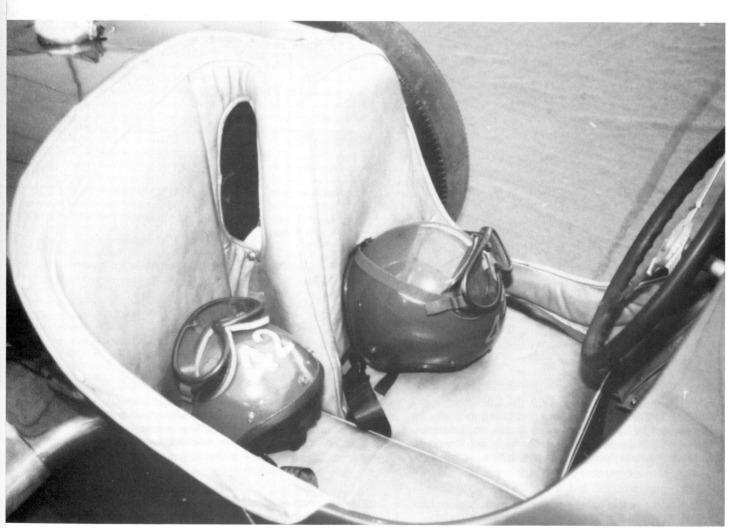

Similar to World Championship Rally co-drivers—but a lot stupider—riding mechanics were a fixture of the sport for many years, but rarely received any credit for their bravery. They were often responsible for hand pumping fuel, changing tires

... and generally acting as a landing pad for the drivers... This may be what remains of the pair launched from this vehicle. Ray Touriel

Details provided by this 1966 photo of Mario Andretti leading the pack to the start show some room for improvements in safety. Note the telephone pole on the outside of the wall, the armco barrier in the background and the blunt end of the pit lane wall. Improvements to racetracks have changed auto racing into a much safer sport. The Milwaukee Mile/Russ Lake

directly to the driver. Often, the car came out of the accident in decent shape, but the driver was severely injured. If the car flipped over, the driver had very little protection. Roll bars were available, but there were almost no regulations governing their design and mounting. Eventually instituted were rules that controlled the structure of the car. But the biggest changes came as USAC began regulating specific components with regard to safety.

"The biggest step forward, in my opinion," Andretti says, "was achieved around the seventies, when they started putting in fuel cells. You know, having those mandatory in the cars really changed the way we looked at the cars. Then, of course, you start looking at some other properties that absorb impact better, such as working with materials between bulkheads and so forth.

"You know, we always thought, 'There's not much you can do to a single seater.' There is not much area to improve, but many times a weight penalty or whatever has to be something that's mandated by the rules. You can always do a little something about the chassis, to the tub, to this and that, but you need other help, too. The ovals are the big problems. The road courses normally have some good run-off and tire barriers [and] a lot of things that you don't have in [ovals]. An oval is a big concrete wall ready to collect a car traveling at a

Al Unser Jr., as pictured in his first season of Indy Car racing in the Coors Light Silver Bullet. Note how far forward Unser sits. The rules have changed regarding the seating position of the driver, forcing designers to move the pedal placement and what's called the footbox behind the axle. Since that move— and the addition of nearly impenetrable carbon fiber footbox construction—the suspension components, which used to pierce the footbox and injure the driver, have been largely kept clear of the drivers legs and feet during crashes. Hank Ives, Havoline Public Relations

tremendous speed. So to me, I'll tell you I think they couldn't get on to something like [changing the fundamental design of the walls] soon enough.

"Unfortunately, there is always a move after an accident. Sometimes, you have to wait for something to really wake you up. Hopefully, we try to bring that wake-up call and say, 'Let's try to avoid that next time; let's try to do something before some of these things happen again. Like [Formula One driver] Piers Courage—it was one that comes to my mind and then the man dies, you know, because he was suffocated by fire. There was nothing wrong physically with him other than that, yet he died. And Swede Savage in Indianapolis is an example; again, he would have survived [with today's fuel safety standards]. An impact tore the car into three pieces, but the fire killed the man. So they addressed that. Some [other] specific examples occurred because we were smart enough to learn from others' mistakes," Andretti said, speaking about accidents that prompted change.

Fire Still a Major Hazard

Fire safety remains a major concern with the Indy Car sanctioning bodies. Although the danger has not been eliminated, there have been only a handful of incidents in the past decade. Each car is fitted with an automatic fire extinguisher system that will deploy in the event of a fire. At the same time, the fuel in the pits is monitored by race officials. If a fire does occur, the team is fined a minimum of $500. Buckets of water sit just on the other side of the pit wall and at least one fire extinguisher in each pit is required. Refueling hoses are dry-break hoses—meaning they will not spill fuel as they are disengaged from the fueling buckeye. Height and capacity of the pit refuelers varies from the Indy 500 to the rest of the circuits, but all are well regulated. The crew must wear fireproof suits during pit stops. In fact, anyone in the pits during the race must wear a fireproof suit,—and the refueling men must wear helmets, or at least goggles, and balaclavas (fireproof hood). Only seven people are allowed over the pit wall at any time during a race or official practice session—six crewmen working on the car and a crewman with pit board.

The days of the driver cruising along in a tee-shirt and goggles are over. Drivers wear suits of Nomex or similar fireproof materials, and full-face helmets, which are often made of carbon fiber. And five- or six-point harnesses keep the driver securely in the car during a race.

In addition, and as we have discussed previously, the car is kept deliberately low-tech. That is often done for safety. For example, the overall dimensions of the car—with attention to the cockpit—is kept fairly large. The extra baggage gives the car some more padding to absorb impacts. At the same time, the driver has been moved backwards so that the "footbox," where the pedals and the driver's feet are located, is behind the front axle. It is also designed so that upon impact, the suspension pieces will deflect rather than entering the footbox and causing injury to the driver's legs.

Weight regulations is an area that has been decidedly—and intentionally—behind the times. The car could certainly be lighter than it is, but race officials feel it would be less safe if the designers were able to trim the weight. Some officials, in fact, feel it is not heavy enough.

"There are some safety features that obviously can be a performance penalty," says Andretti, "and that's why you sometimes need to add weight. If you make the weight mandatory, then the engineers have to just figure it in, but it is equal for everyone. So there is no engineer in this world who would come forward and argue against it. They have spent a lot of energy and time making the cars safer, but their big concern is with how to make the car just go fast. You need an organized approach and then you need a sanctioning body to follow up. With the drivers' push to make these safety features mandatory, they have turned up in [the newer designs], and that's what we have achieved over the years.

"Bringing the speed for the cars down is being addressed every year. It's just that there is no easy way to do it. A lot of people have a tendency to have this quick answer, 'Oh, take the wings off', or something like that. But if you do, you realize that the only way you are slowing the car down is making it tricky. The car becomes unbalanced, making it tough to drive, which means that you are going to have more accidents. Like, for instance, we used to go to the Phoenix season opener, and—man!—I used to have 10 X's on the wall. Bang, bang, bang, bang, bang.

"Even drivers make some stupid statements like, 'Why don't we go flat bottom?' They don't realize that [a] flat-bottom car is going to fly like a matchbox, you know, like if you go sideways at the speeds we're going. It works in Formula One because they have more down force than we do. But even then, it's a terrible type of down force because it comes unstuck very easily."

Safety Team Ready to Respond

When all has been done properly and a crash still occurs, the only thing CART and USAC can do is try to dispatch a professional to the scene as soon as possible. At Indy—and most tracks on the circuit—that means a safety crew truck will be rolling even before the car comes to a stop.

The race series' safety team was established in 1984 as a response to two accidents at the Michigan

The look of Indy Car has changed a great deal since this photo of Al Unser in his Lola T8600 was taken in 1986. The cars have gone on a diet, and the overall design now stresses com- *pactness. The result is a much smaller, slimmer car.* Hank Ives, Havoline Public Relations

Always ready, hopefully bored, fire fighters wait for what they hope won't occur. The crash that killed Dave MacDonald and Eddie Sachs at Indianapolis in 1964 prompted strict fuel safety regulations. Gravity feed systems were instituted as the only form of re-fueling—a regulation that exists today.

Thick, wide webbing for harnesses ensures the driver will not be thrown from the cockpit in a crash. This type of safety equipment is a far cry from a polo shirt and leather helmet, the type of gear of drivers in the early days of the sport. Despite outstanding modern safety harnesses, risks remain. For instance, Paul Tracy's harnesses came unbuckled during the running of the season finale at Laguna Seca in 1993. Tracy was leading the race when his belts came undone, and he had to decide whether to carry on or pull into the pits so he could slow down enough to reach for the buckle and re-secure himself. A true racer, Tracy drove on and won the race, but noted that he experienced remarkable lifting out of the seat of the car during decents on the hilly course.

500 in 1981. Twenty-three professionals and six specially equipped vehicles stand ready and waiting throughout the three days of any weekend and the month of May to deal with any injuries that may occur. And at any race, there is a mobile trauma center, a vehicle and facility valued at $750,000. The 40ft custom motor coach can treat several severely injured patients simultaneously. There are also a pair of golf-cart sized ambulances called MR-10s that patrol the back of the pit lane, and each is staffed by a physician.

So not all the changes have to come with the cars. In fact, some of the best advances in safety come from the tracks themselves. Concrete replaces

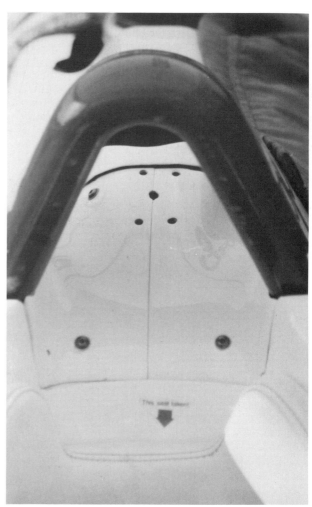

The roll bar, uncovered. Ernest Hemingway once said race car driving and bull fighting were the only two true sports. The similarities between the two speak for themselves—but bullfighters no longer have tech inspectors and safety commissions. Today's roll bars double as loops for tow trucks to hook on and lift disabled cars off the track after breakdowns or mishaps. There's nothing less pleasing for a driver than to see his car on the end of the hook, a signal that, for him, the race is over.

The roll bar must exceed (rise above) the driver's helmet by 5in, as this one on Danny Sullivan car clearly does. Should the car roll over, it will theoretically still clear his helmet. It works, too. Just ask Rick Mears, who ended up upside-down during a practice crash at Indianapolis in the final year of his career as a driver. He ended up wirh scrapes on his helmet, but the car came to rest on its roll bar, not on him.

armco or steel railings to avoid injury that comes from the driver's limbs striking the metal barrier. Sand traps replace tire barriers. Runoff room has increased a great deal over the years.

"I think the best reasonable move is to come up with some kind of energy-absorbing walls for the ovals and superspeedways," Andretti says. "These days, for us, anything is a superspeedway, because the speeds that we reach in the mile ovals are just tremendous. Oval track operators could commission three or four top industrial engineering firms and could come up with an answer here. And then award the work to whoever is selected. There may eventually have to be a barrier in front of the walls that will give some upon impact. Obviously, you don't want the car to stop dead or to collect the car when you just brush it or to come apart.

"There has been some study after several crashes; one was Jeff's [Mario's son Jeff Andretti] for instance. He went head on into the wall [at Indy] when the wheel came off, and he nailed that wall at almost a dead-straight angle. You know, he pulled, like, 58 Gs. How he survived, that is a big question, but General Motors studied that and said if there could've been any kind of a collapsible structure to soften the initial impact to some degree—like, if it could've given 7, 8, 10, 12in—he probably could have walked away with half his injuries.

"The carbon fiber [of the race car] did give. But, you know, that can only do so much. An example that I always used is when I was watching a NASCAR car race at Dover [in 1992]. Derrike Cope came off turn four, and he had one of those long spins. Now, he had never touched the outer wall, but by the time he gathered it up, he went head on into the pit wall. The wall was very narrow and looked very dangerous. But it had an energy-absorbing point to it. I think it had some steel in it, but what I'm saying is that when he hit the wall, it gave quite a bit. You know, he gave an interview 5min later. If that wall would've been as solid as the outside wall, the way he hit, I guarantee that his eyes would have come out of his head. So that makes sense to me as the next step."

John Andretti and the ominous-looking fireproof balaclava. Anyone in the pits during the race must wear a fireproof suit— and the refueling men must wear helmets, or at least goggles, and balaclavas.

But safety is relative. How safe can you be at 240mph? Critics say that the safer the cars get, the faster the drivers want to go, and the faster they go, the more they crash and the worse the crashes. Did Andretti feel that speeds had crept up farther than they needed to go? In other words, were people going for it more?

"Just because safety comes into the sport, no, it does not make you take any more risks. You know, I take as many risks now as I did then. You don't think about those things when you are there. You think about it before and then after, but you don't think about when you are doing it."

Racing is still a dangerous sport, but unlike the early days, it is not a reckless one. That a driver can be one of a field of men and women who have survived some thirty years says a great deal about where the sport has come. The fields get older because they *can* get older. Attrition is no longer a way to become a veteran. In the final analysis, yes, racing has its danger, but it still moves forward, not backwards.

"Everything's got a problem today," Andretti says. "Yes, it's being addressed. They just theoretically eliminated 25 percent of downforce from [1992-1993], but today's technology gets it all back now. As soon as you do anything about it, it changes that much further; you go that much faster. Sometimes, just by keeping the cars about the same speed, you could say, 'Mission accomplished'."

This is not just any helmet, this is the helmet of thirty-year veteran Mario Andretti. Not only are today's helmets protective,
they're also extremely aerodynamic. The V-shaped protrusions
near the top of Andretti's helmet help direct the wind over his
head and minimize the buffeting he will experience at the high
speeds of today's racing. Some helmets are no longer rounded
in the rear; instead, they're flatter, a move that also improves
air flow and minimizes drag and buffeting.

Chapter 13

Sum of the Parts: The Indy Car Package

The process of racing can be overwhelming. Not specifically the racing, since drivers and teams, by necessity, must love the racing. But the show, in general, can be an insidious process that emotionally overburdens some in the traveling circus.

Most weeks during the season, it begins on Friday. If it's the month of May and the teams are at Indianapolis, it will start on Monday morning.

At more than half the season's racetracks—at ten of sixteen races—weather conditions will not matter in the slightest; the show still will go on, rain or shine, on the road courses. In May, at the Indianapolis Motor Speedway, or at Phoenix, Michigan, or any of the other ovals, rain means waiting, anticipating, hoping.

Hope springs eternal in racing. It's what gets a driver on the pole for the race or simply in the field. It is what helps him make the pass under braking; ultimately, it was what got him the ride with the team in the first place. It is part of the show. For some, it is the show. It is preparation more than anything. The race is a series of events, perhaps, that, with a great deal of luck, can yield a winner who wasn't expected to be a factor. But the first days of the weekend is when the fast drivers shine.

The apprehension of the start is as powerful as the apprehension of the finish. The preparation shows the potential, the potential for Sunday—or for the next Sunday or for a Sunday sometime in the future. Preparation to win. That win is undefinable. It could be a victory Sunday or a good qualifying run; it could be the satisfaction of a good finish, the satisfaction of a win, or perhaps it is the championship that looms on the horizon. Perhaps it is a race for sponsorship dollars—as long as the show is good, the money will flow. Different races for different reasons. One goal is common: They want to do their best.

"There is always apprehension," says Indy Car regular Dominic Dobson, "because there is a desire to do well. You put pressure on yourself; you want to perform well and not make mistakes."

For some, fear is a motivator—especially at Indy.

"The biggest thing that happens to an Indy Car driver," Dobson says, "is when they call racers to the starting line of the Indy 500 on race day or even a weekend to qualify. There are so many people there that every other racetrack seems to pale in comparison. Once you've been in the starting line at Indy, nothing else looks like a crowd."

Compared to the season's "normal" weeks and months, the month of May is an entirely different process. It is at once more drawn out with more time to define the race car and the track and more intense, with pressure always present. The average event is a three-day affair that obliges participants to get their best in just under 55 hours from start to finish.

So the event begins Friday morning at every track except the Brickyard. The desolate place that is a racetrack comes alive with activity. The teams have arrived Thursday evening and the cars have been unloaded. The trailers have been turned into a small technopolis, complete with every possible tool that can make a car quicker. The driver will be prepared, and at 9:30 a.m., the first practice will begin.

Feeling Out the Car and the Track

If the car has a new engine or a fresh rebuild, the driver will do one or two laps easy and then come in on for an "assistance check." He will have kept the car at about 5000-7000rpm, perhaps running it up to 10,000 once. As he returns to the pits, he will shut it down. Cover off, the crew will check the fittings to make sure the oil lines, water lines, and cables are fitted properly. If everything is OK, the engine cover will be replaced and the driver will go back out—this time, for maybe ten laps, just to establish how the tracks feels.

Is it dirty? Clean? Is there any rubber down? Is the car going to bottom out anywhere? Ride height is important, and the driver will want to get the car down as far as he can have it. He will want to feel the balance of the car. Does it understeer? Oversteer? How much grip does it have?

The driver is interpreting the track for the members of the crew, who do their best to get him a better setup. But the equation is so complicated. Grip can be related to tires, suspension, or aerodynamics—or a combination of all three. The driver must sort out some of the input to give the crew a decent diagnosis.

Nothing ever looks together until the car makes it to the track Friday. The trailers will have been turned into a small technopolis, complete with every possible tool that can make a car quicker. The driver will be prepared and at 9:30 a.m., the first practice will begin.

Transporter city: The moveable Indy Car show is like a home away from home. After every race the tent city is disassembled and the gear is packed snugly away, prepared for the next *race at the next circuit. Somewhere else, another deserted circuit prepares for activity, and inconspicuously the caravan travels that direction.*

Three ten-lap runs later, and they hope they're taking the right direction. They want to keep making progress all the way through the weekend. If they ever go backwards, chances are slim they will ever make it back. The initial setup will be the foundation for later.

The driver will go out several times during the first session, usually in five- to ten-lap spurts. He'll begin trying to find the fast way around the track, finding the braking points and the areas that hold advantages for his style of driving. He'll file the facts away in his head, saving them for qualifying.

At the break between Friday's 1.5hr practice and the first qualifying session, drivers may be doing practice laps in their heads, trying to determine where they can find that extra tenth of a second. The time in their heads should exactly match the time on the practice sheets. If they make time internally, they will reduce the time on the sheets as well.

The crew will work on the car while the driver continues searching his mind for the elusive "tenth." Perhaps the ride height will be changed again, maybe a flat or a couple of flats—less than one-third of a turn of the nut makes that much difference.

Qualification is done in two groups at road courses, usually with the faster cars running first on Friday and last on Saturday. At oval tracks, qualifying will be done in single car timed laps. Either way, on Friday it's only provisional, and drivers will have another shot at it Saturday. If something goes wrong Saturday, they might have to go home, so they try their best to put the car in the top end of the grid.

Some drivers are very quick right off the bat, and others take a long time to get acquainted to qualifying speeds. First qualifying begins with trepidation, and during the first few laps of the half-hour, most drivers will run in even shorter stints than in the first practice: three, four laps—one lap out of the pits, two flying laps, and a cool lap.

In that lap or two, the driver should be able to feel whatever change was made last. Was there is an improvement? The final answer is not in the car, but on the stopwatch.

"The car tells you in two ways if you are fast," Dobson says. "One is by feeling the car; if it feels better, it might not necessarily be better because lap time and feel do not always correspond. Most times, if the car feels better, it's going to go faster, but

The transporter holds just about every possible spare part the crew could need. The split level holds two cars, spare engines, and serves as a self-contained workshop.

sometimes the car will feel better to you and will go slower, and you make a change and the car feels worse or a little more nervous or harder to drive, but you actually go quicker."

At one time, drivers who had poor qualifying results would work on the race setup rather than focus on something as useless as the starting grid. But as the field becomes more competitive, it becomes more difficult to pass. So qualifying position, even in a 2hr race, is critical.

Perhaps the effort was good enough; maybe it was disappointing. Possibly, it didn't happen at all; maybe the car failed to make the field. Either way, the crew will work on mechanical setup of the car overnight, checking spring rates, damping, shocks and roll bars. The gears will be changed out of the transmission in the evening. On a high-speed track, aerodynamic concerns will be addressed.

A Change of Engines

The teams would likely show up on Friday with the engine that was run in the last race. So Friday night—or perhaps Saturday night—the team will change the power plant, replacing it with a fresh one for the morning's practice. Each engine is a sealed unit, and the crew won't fiddle with it other than possibly changing spark plugs or oil. The gearing might be changed if it is not quite right. During the day, the difference is not great enough to prompt a change, but with the time at night, the gearbox may be renovated. Basic maintenance will be undertaken; general cleaning and inspections will take place. The brake rotors will likely be changed

Bobby Rahal's "T" car (training car defined by its "X" marking). Switching to the T car during the weekend is a traumatic experience for some drivers. Practicing in the regular race car the majority of the weekend makes it difficult to tune the back-up car with as much precision as the primary car.

On the first day of practice, the driver does more waiting for the crew to adjust the car than he does driving. Cars are thoroughly inspected for worn parts and potential failures during the weeks between races. Everything's reassembled for race weekend, and it's almost like starting over; last weekend's winning car might not run like a champ at the start of this week's practice.

again; the suspension and turbo will be examined in detail.

The 1hr Saturday morning session begins at 9:30. The driver will determine how the overnight changes worked in the entire package. The session is treated a little bit like Friday, full of five-lap tests, then in for a check. The warm-up will be abandoned, and the driver will go straight for an exploratory run. What is the car doing, how sensitive is the set up?

"Sometimes, you can't get both ends of the car working as well as you like them," says Dobson, "so you actually have to remove some down force on one end. Let's say for example you got a second gear turn or a third gear turn and the car is very loose. It oversteers too much. You've done what you can on the rear, but you see you've got the wing all the way up so you've got maximum down force. Then you've got to take some down force away from the front because what's happening is that the front is sticking too well and is hooking the car around the corner. So understanding the relation-ship between the mechanical aspects of the car and the aerodynamic aspects is something that drivers have to learn."

The engineer will ask, "Which corner?" The corners, which are divided up into three parts—entry, middle, and exit—describe perfectly how the car reacts. Therein lies the key to the elusive perfect setup. Get a variety of corners perfect, and the car will be as close to ideal as it can get.

By the end of Saturday morning's session, most changes would have tended to be conservative. No dramatic changes have occurred yet. After the first session Saturday, the team might get desperate and make radical changes. Usually, it will be fruitless at that point; on rare occasions, a huge change will work. Generally, by that time, teams will simply be fishing. On an oval, a radical change can mean a losing bout with the retaining wall.

The driver will be looking to go a little quicker than in the first practice. The tuning is fine. Perhaps there is a slight understeer that wasn't detected before. The speeds are rising, and the circumstances have changed. More rubber is down, but it might be more slippery. The heat may have brought the oils up out of the track. The weather is a variable that will play havoc with the gains made up to that point. The morning session would have been fairly cool. Is the track better or worse? Is there understeer in the fast corner? Can the team pick up a little grip by lowering the car or taking air out of the tires? Is it better or worse?

Any driver will likely have improved each time out, but typically everybody else did, too. So the half-second one driver has gained is nullified as everyone else makes the same gains. Things will have been clear Friday afternoon: Typically, the driver who was twenty-second on Friday will not be able to jump to fifth on Saturday. The slow guys get quicker and the quick guys get quicker.

"You may see people getting a little desperate if they're struggling," Dobson says. "But most people will work incrementally at improving the car, based on the information they have. It depends on how well you've done. If you've qualified well on Friday—let's say you're in the top ten and you're comfortable with that—Saturday, you might want to work on your race setup.

"The driver might want to run full tanks on Saturday morning. Typically, teams wait until Sunday morning to run full tanks, but there are drivers who don't always qualify who are always there in the race. Someone like Little Al is a good example; you know, he's never been a strong qualifier. He's always there; he's always in the top ten, but he's comfortable having qualified seventh or eighth or whatever, but in the race he's almost always right there be-

If the car has a new engine or one that's been freshly rebuilt, the driver will do one or two easy laps, then come in for an "assistance check." He will have kept the car at around 5000-7000rpm, perhaps running it up to 10,000 once. As he re-turns to the pits, he will shut it down. Cover off, the crew will check the fittings to make sure the oil lines, water lines, and cables are fitted properly. If everything is fine, the engine cover will be replaced and the driver will go back out.

cause I think he always concentrates on his race set-up and is more concerned with Sunday than the grid position. He may do longer runs, too. He may run twenty laps in a row, for example, on Saturday morning just to see how the car behaves and how the fuel runs out."

Qualifying: The Pressure is On

Each driver is different. And regardless of the strategy, Saturday afternoon's qualifying session will determine the qualifying position for the race. Or, as the Indy Car grids fill up with the series becoming increasingly popular, a driver will be in the position of making the race or not making the race. It's a time of intense pressure.

"I like to spend a little time by myself before qualifying," says Dobson, "trying to think of where I can pick up a tenth of a second here or a tenth of a second there. Maybe do some laps mentally in my head prior to going out there. You might take some risks Saturday afternoon that you previously hadn't. You'd let it hang out a little bit. You might brake a little bit deeper or whatever."

If a driver was going to have an "off,"—where they spin off or simply go off the track—Saturday afternoon's probably when it's going to happen. Everybody is trying very hard. How difficult it is to improve two-tenths of a second at this point. Those two-tenths could move the car up five spots on the grid. It could be the difference between the pole and fifth, or the difference between twentieth and fifteenth. A half-second covers the first fifteen spots at most grids.

So the driver sucks it up and goes perhaps a little faster than he should. Some drivers want to scare themselves every lap. The heart monitors show the nerves: Heart rates climb to 160 beats per minute.

"I don't call it fear. I don't think that constantly scaring myself is the way to improve my performance," Dobson comments. "Some drivers are a little different. It could be that a driver is mentally wired that way, so he needs to scare himself every corner. I think of myself as, 'Am I pushing myself to the limit? Is there any place where I felt I left anything on the table?' I want to go through every corner on my qualifying lap knowing that there isn't

The cover comes off again. There's not necessarily anything wrong, but the crew does its normal Friday maintenance. The driver is interpreting the track for the crew members, who do their best to get him a better set-up. Grip can be related to tires, suspension, or aerodynamics—or a combination of all three. The driver must sort out some of the input to give the crew a decent diagnosis of how the car's performing and where it needs adjustments.

On-board air jacks are utilized every time the car is on pit road, with the air supply coming through the hose attached to the fitting atop the car. In the paddock, ordinary hydraulic floor jacks are used. Christian Dannaer's car sits on its air jacks between practice runs.

anything left there to be had. Call it fear, call it performing well, I don't know. But I don't go through the corner thinking, 'Christ, am I going to get through this thing, or am I gong to die trying?'"

Then he thinks about it.

"If you're talking about qualifying at Indianapolis, you bump that apprehension up. Talk about a pressure cooker situation. There's nothing like the four laps of qualifying for the Indy 500. I would say that the fear of 'Am I going to make it through the corner OK?' is probably higher there than at any other racetrack. But the fact is, you don't have to do just one good lap at Indy, you have to do four in a row. And if you screw up one corner in four laps, you can potentially screw up your whole qualifying attempt. So I sort of feel you wouldn't approach each corner at Indy four corners in a row wondering if I am going to live to see the exit. If that's what it

took, I'd probably get out of the game. But I go into the corner thinking, 'I know that last time when I came in here the car was right at the very edge. Can I go into it faster?'. Probably not. 'If I turned into it and kept my foot flat and the car drove up to the wall, within a half-inch of the wall, can I go through it any faster? Probably not. If I tried, I'd probably cross over from being brave into being stupid.' You've seen drivers do that at Indy."

At a road course, things are different. Speeds are lower. The driver has time to react. If the car does snap sideways, the chances of catching it are much better on a road course. "If the car snaps sideways at Indy, you're done for," says Dobson. "You don't have that luxury of catching it."

The qualifying effort is finished. The team will make minor adjustments to the car. If major changes are made, it is because the team has done a

Waiting made easier. The front runners may be surrounded at the track by autograph seekers, Spandex-clad women, or at least an orchestrated effort of uniformed public relations people. Eric Bachelart doesn't have the fame for that yet.

dismal job in the first two days. If that's the case, most likely they will not be a factor in the race's outcome.

A big overnight change for Saturday is a replacement of all four springs or all four shocks. The engine may be changed again, depending on the cycle of replacement set by the engine suppliers. Major replacements may occur; major changes will not.

Sunday: Race Day

Sunday morning starts early. The crowds at the track will double. Even getting to the track will be difficult at some places. For quite a while, Indy Cars did not practice on Sundays. But now, the drivers get one final look at the track—except at Indy, where the drivers will not have seen the circuit since the previous Thursday.

Tanks will be full Sunday morning—or more full, at any rate. Most will be running with at least 20gal. They might scrub another set of tires in preparation for the race; they might bed another set of brake pads, or even bed some brake rotors. They might check the ring and pinion gears again. Ride height might be adjusted one more time. The driver will take it out for a few flyers.

Seasoned fans know that the morning warm-up tells it all. If one team has qualified fifteenth, but was third-quickest in the morning warm-up, it might be indicative of how the day will go for them. Maybe they took a gamble and made some changes; perhaps the changes paid off and Sunday morning the car was much better. They would want to establish a time, like setting an agenda.

Teams will start the race with three sets of scrubbed tires. The race will start on the tires the team used to qualify. All the work will hopefully pay off. All the possibilities will unfold as the team waits for the command to start engines. The apprehension will mount. Drivers do different things, have different rituals.

"I don't like sitting in the car for 10min before the 'Start engines,' so I like to be comfortably in a couple of minutes before," says Dobson. "I close my visor and just kind of shut myself off from people and think about the start."

The race begins to take shape and the cars get the starter's orders. "You'll get your engine started, get off the line OK," Dobson says. "In your parade laps, it's important to get your tires warm. That's when you see all your scrubbing back and forth. You want to put some heat into the tires and you want to put some heat into the engine, into the turbo, and into the brakes. So you kind of drag the brakes with your left foot maybe, and run the engine a little harder than you would to maintain just a pace. You'll be checking your gauges, making sure that temperatures are OK and that there are no problems. You can only assume that it's going to be the

same as it was that morning, because you've done that."

The weekend has built itself into a crescendo that does not culminate at the end of the race, but at the beginning. It is like a huge party—a wedding—where the event itself is bigger than the result.

"You stay up with the group," Dobson explains. "You don't want to be left behind. Sometimes on the road courses, you come out for the green flag and if you're sleeping—not literary but figuratively—you find yourself half a lap down. If there's a tight corner before the green flag and you are not there pushing the guy in front of you, then all you need is

Big crowds for a Saturday in California, but nothing compared to Indianapolis. Laguna Seca consistently attracts larger crowds each season for its season-ending Indy car race. Thousands flocked to the track on this day to watch qualifying for the Indy Car race and to be treated to races of other race groups such as Indy Lights or Trans-Am.

One of the many ways to package spares. This mini-trailer contains mostly electronic equipment which will be used as a link to the car while it's on the track. After a practice run, systems numbers might be crunched and scrutinized on these screens before adjustments are made.

a two- or three-car gap, and you compound that all the way back. If you start in the back of the pack, the guys are in the third turn before you get the green flag."

The pole sitter sets the pace to the starting line and everyone else follows. The driver who qualified second and who starts on the outside in the front row is responsible to stay even with, but not get ahead of, the pole sitter. If the second-best qualifier goes faster than the pole sitter, the starter has the option of calling off the start. Then the field takes another lap and tries again.

The Start Raises Many Questions

The start is a mass of questions. What's the strategy? Will the driver behind try to make up ground on the start or will he be conservative? Will there be contact? Will someone be unlucky?

Before the race, the drivers will have had a strategy meeting with the crews. The start will be discussed, as well as the overall strategy for the event. The pre-race briefing with all engineers will yield a pit window, a three-lap opening where the driver

The cars come to the grid on Sunday, race day. Based on the car's performance in qualifying, teams will have a good idea of how competitive they will be in the race itself. If a team has no realistic chance of winning, it may set other performance goals to see if it can improve upon its previous performances—building blocks to a possible win down the road. The more teams there are who can field truly competitive entries, the better for the race circuit and the fans.

Team owner Roger Penske (right) and driver Nigel Mansell share a few words together. This photo was taken at Laguna Seca in 1992, the season prior to Mansell's historic debut in Indy Car racing. In fact, this was his first appearance at an Indy Car road race. One season later, Penske's drivers would be chasing Mansell for the season points crown.

will need to pit for fuel. If there is a yellow caution period, less fuel would have been used, and fuel mileage calculations change. A fuel meter in the car tells the driver how much fuel he is using. If that fails, a crew man has a pit board that tells him the number as the laps tick off. The telemetry system sends the signal back to the pits, where they can monitor fuel. The driver won't want to think about it; that's the engineer's job or the team manager's job. The driver's job is to watch the gear shifts, check the temperature gauge once a lap if possible, or maybe just on the straight-away. And, oh yes, race.

"Generally you are pretty busy," says Dobson. "If you are racing, sometimes you might not look at your temperature gauges for three or four laps if you

The Andrettis—as they were in 1992. The father-son team of Mario (right) and Michael was very successful under the Newman-Haas banner. Nevertheless, at this writing the "Andretti curse" has kept both men out of the Indianapolis 500 winner's circle in recent years. Michael has won the season championship and led throughout most of an Indy 500, but gremlins and bad luck have so far kept him from the Speedway's winner's circle.

Bobby Rahal waits for the start. The three-time Indy Car champion and 1986 Indy 500 winner always seems to be in the hunt for the championship.

Al Unser, Jr., is relaxed before a race. He's wearing the Galles-Kraco uniform he sported prior to joining Roger Penske's team for the 1994 season. His driver's suit and full-face helmet are a far cry from driver gear of yesteryear, which consisted of short-sleeved shirts and perhaps a kerchief over the face to fight the dust. Second and even third generation drivers are fairly common in motor racing; ones as successful as Indy 500 winner and Indy car champion Al Jr. are not.

Dominic Dobson smiles before qualifying at Indianapolis. "There is always apprehension," the Indy car regular says, "because there is desire to do well. You put pressure on yourself. You want to perform well and not make mistakes."

The car awaits Mario. The small white box sticking out to the left of the roll bar is the in-car camera; the small dark space on the box is the lens opening. His helmet is designed to be as aerodynamically efficient as possible. The small tab sticking out to the right of his helmet is the pull tab for the visor tear-off; one-by-one, layers of these plastic tear-offs are disposed of as they get dirty during a race.

Jimmy Vasser and Mike Groff wait in their cars for the race to start. Some drivers prefer to wait until the last minute before getting in the cars. "I don't like sitting in the car for ten minutes before the 'start engines.' I like to be comfortably in [there] a couple of minutes before," says Dominic Dobson. "I close my visor and just kind shut myself off from people and think about the start."

are engaged in a battle with someone that you are really racing. So a lot of systems now have an alarm where there are preset parameters—the oil pressure drops down at a certain point or the water temperature gets at a certain point—and it just flashes an alarm on the dash and it catches your attention. You really don't have to monitor it. As long as your alarm doesn't come on, you know that you're OK. You might check your boost to make sure that's not flipping, because that's something we want to keep right at 45in. The fact of the matter is that if your water temperature starts going up and your oil pressure starts going down, that's indicative that there is a major problem with your engine and it's probably going to blow up. There's not much you can do about it. Your options are to keep going until it does blow up or pull in the pits and end your day. You know, slowing down and taking it easy nowadays isn't really an option."

Hearing the Racing Gremlins

As the laps tick down, the driver will begin to hear rattles and grumbles and feel vibrations that weren't there before. Some of the sounds are nonexistent. Others are simply magnified by an imagination running wild. At the same time, the fact is that by the end of a 400-mile race, the strain will have taken its toll on the car. Things really *may* be deteriorating inside the engine or transmission.

If there really is a noise, do you stop?

"If I was hearing a noise and there were ten laps to go and I can race for position or I can back off and maintain a position," Dobson says, "I [would] probably consult with my engineer or my crew member or chief mechanic and say, 'I'm hearing some funny [noise] out the engine.' When you start hearing a noise, well, that's an immediate signal to check your gauges. You know, these kind of motors don't give you any warning. If they are going to blow up, they just blow up. They don't start to go and then fifty laps later finally go. They might give you a warning; you might hear it two to three laps and then it goes."

The responses vary. Some drivers stay out until

MARIO ANDRETTI
2 Kmart/HAVOLINE LOLA-FORD
PIT CREW ASSIGNMENTS

(Australia, Phoenix, Indianapolis, Milwaukee, New Hampshire, Michigan, Cleveland, Vancouver, Mid-Ohio, Nazareth, Laguna Seca)

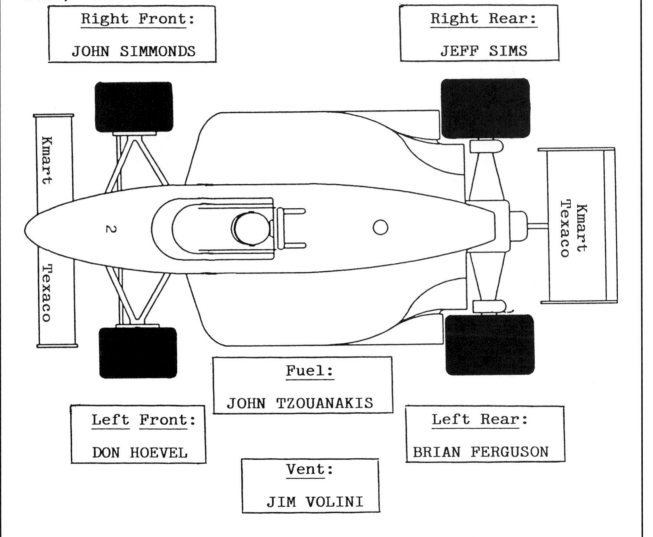

Right Front:
JOHN SIMMONDS

Right Rear:
JEFF SIMS

Kmart Texaco

Kmart Texaco

Fuel:
JOHN TZOUANAKIS

Left Front:
DON HOEVEL

Left Rear:
BRIAN FERGUSON

Vent:
JIM VOLINI

Chief Mechanic: Carl Dean (radio to driver)
Engineer: Brian Lisles
Board Man: Ken Kirkpatrick
Dead-Man Valve: (changes each race)
Telemetry and Electronics: Tim Wise
Timing and Scoring: Berni Haas and Cathy Beadle

This chart shows the 1992 crew that would go over the wall for Mario Andretti. Six people go over the wall: one on each wheel, a fuel man, and a vent man. The chief mechanic stays in touch with the driver via radio, informing him of his position, his lap times, the times of other drivers, and his fuel situation. With the help of track spotters who watch from a variety of vantage points, information about effective lines through turns and debris or incidents ahead can be relayed to the driver as well.

The starter is always available. Should the driver stall the car in the pits during his stop, the crew will quickly move toward an external starter such as this one to re-fire the motor.

the car explodes. Some drivers back off just enough to make it to the end of the race. "But racers being racers," continues Dobson, "I think most guys will gamble and take their chances at the end."

By the end of the race, if the driver has had a good run, he will be happy. Again, that may not be a win. It may simply be a finish. The driver and crew will be exhausted. No matter what, the job has been done to the best of the participants' abilities.

"You congratulate your crew. If they've done a good job, you might offer to take them out. But you first need to sit down with your engineers to talk about the car, how it performed. Let's say, for example, it was understeering on full tanks and it was getting loose as the fuel went down; or maybe your second set of tires was no good and the car was really sliding around a lot, but then the third lap picked up. That's good information to go over with your engineer after the race. It's important to get it out while it is fresh in your mind because that's information that can help you the next event. Then you pack it up and do it all over again the next weekend."

The tent city is disassembled and the gear is packed snugly away, prepared for the next race at the next circuit. The racetrack reverts back to its regular austere and desolate condition, the magazines, newspapers, and video tape supplying the only evidence that something special had occurred. Somewhere else, another deserted circuit prepares for activity. And inconspicuously, the caravan travels in that direction.

The process begins as the procession moves. The pressure mounts, the anticipation returns. Will the package be better at the next track? One thing is certain: everyone will do their best to make it so.

Emerson Fittipaldi uncharacteristically runs over the rumble strips. Fatigue will affect the drivers during a race. Fittipaldi is known for being preoccupied with his diet and overall fitness.

He does extensive weight training and endurance work to stay in shape. Even so, a hard race takes its toll on the human body.

Mario Andretti (shown in 1993) is a veteran driver who is still competitive after decades in the sport. 1994 was to be his final season. He had proven a fierce competitor and leader off-track as well.

Dominic Dobson at speed at Indy. Compare his car's speedway set-up to the road course set-up of Mario Andretti's car in the previous photo. By comparison, Dobson's car has extremely small wings, front and rear. The back side of his helmet is not rounded; instead, it's shaped for optimum aerodynamic performance amid the winds that will swirl about his cockpit. Imagine the car with no suspension, wheels, or tires and you can picture it as a rocket capable of flight.

When the race is over the crew loads the car back on the truck and takes it away to the next track—where the process starts all over again.

Chapter 14

Dissection of the Modern Indy Car

Chassis

Lola T9300 (speedway setup shown): Carbon fiber composite and honeycomb aluminum, with conservative undertray venturis, or ground effects.

Wheelbase: 113.5in (111.5in road course wheelbase available)

Weight: 1,525lb, including lubricant and coolant, excluding fuel

Weight distribution: 45 percent front/55 percent rear

Track: 78.5in front/80.5in rear

Length: 185in

Height: 32in

Width: 78.5in

Width of cockpit: 18x30in

Front Wing: Carbon fiber, incorporating the nose cone; amount of wing exposure producing up to 1,500lb of down force

Front Suspension: Push rod, actuated by rockers; inboard springs and dampers, adjustable anti-roll bar

Steering: Rack-and-pinion, ratio adjustable to 1:1 lock-to-lock

Front Wheels: 15in diameter cast-magnesium, supplied by Lola

Front Tires: 25.5x9.5in Goodyear Eagle Speedway radials

Brakes: Iron discs, with pre-bedded carbon metallic pads, cast or billeted alloy with six calipers

Sidepods/Bodywork: Fiberglass with select parts formed of carbon fiber, containing one radiator on each side

Data Download Port: Informational only; no changes can be made through computer. Electronically records performance of engine and actuation of controls by driver, in real time, lap-by-lap, or download capacity; used as a foundation for determining setup

Fuel Tank: Goodyear Tire and Rubber ballistic flexible bladder; 40gal capacity, with two fuel pickups; filler valve buckeyes located on either side, using only one per race, and vented at the top

Fuel: Methanol (wood alcohol)

Rear Suspension

Rear Suspension: Push rod, actuated by rockers; inboard springs and dampers, adjustable anti-roll bar

Rear Wheels: 15in diameter cast-magnesium, 14.5in width, supplied by Lola

Rear Tires: 25.5x14.5in Goodyear Eagle Speedway radials

Rear Wing: Carbon fiber, attached to transmission housing, with wing surface exposure producing up to 3000lb of down force. Limited to 43in overall width and 32in height (35in for road course wings), with a maximum of three elements (at road courses)

Cockpit

Seat: Form-fitted, padded foam

Safety Harness: 3in-wide webbing, tensile strength of 8,000lb, six-point hitch with central disconnect buckle

Gear Shift: Six-speed linkage on ovals; five-speed on road courses

Turbo Boost Knob: Manually actuated via dash; four vacuum lines

Sway Bar Adjustment: Lever control changes bias and tension on each, front and rear

Brake Balance: Knob-actuated, can adjust brake balance from front to rear

Fuel Mix: Richer to leaner mix to control engine heat and fuel economy

Steering Wheel: Contains two-way radio transmit button, gauge readout switch

Gauges: Digital, with the ability for driver to click through a series on screen to check rpm, mph, oil pressure, water temperature, and fuel mileage

Engine

Chevrolet Ilmor Indy C: 161.5in displacement (2647ccm) 80 degree turbocharged V-8 (based on the maximum engine size regulation), 22.8in height, 22in width, 22.1in length

An Indy Car in cut-away view.

Lubrication System: Dry sump, 68psi pressure system
Cooling: Liquid-cooled, centrifugal pump, with sealant only, run from the block up through the engine and through side-mounted radiator
Crankshaft: Forged alloy steel
Connecting Rods: Machined alloy aluminum
Block: Sand-cast aluminum, with wet liners
Pistons: Forged-aluminum alloy
Heads: Sand-cast aluminum alloy
Valves: Four valves per cylinder
Camshafts: Dual overhead cams, four total, gear-driven
Ignition: Individual cylinder coils, electronic
Engine Management: Delco Gen-II
Turbocharger: Garrett Turbo, set at a boost pressure of 45in of mercury, not intercooled (regulation)
Popoff Valve: Set in coordination with 45in boost (regulation) to allow extra boost pressure to escape
Clutch: Three-plate diaphragm spring, pedal-actuated
Transmission: Six-speed, furnished by Lola

Performance
Horsepower: 800-850hp at 12,800rpm
Torque: 375ft-lb at 8800rpm
Top speed: 240mph
0-60: 2sec; 0-100: 4sec

Index